classroom evaluation
for teachers

ISSUES AND INNOVATIONS IN EDUCATION

Consulting Editor
JOSEPH C. BENTLEY
The University of Utah

Expanding the Self: Personal Growth for Teachers— *Angelo V. Boy and Gerald J. Pine, University of New Hampshire*

Changing Student Behavior: A New Approach to Discipline—*Duane Brown, West Virginia University*

Classroom Evaluation for Teachers—*Henry Dizney, University of Oregon*

Compensatory Programming: The Acid Test of American Education—*Joe L. Frost, The University of Texas at Austin, and G. Thomas Rowland, The Institute for Epistemic Studies*

Educational Media and the Teacher—*John B. Haney, University of Illinois at Chicago Circle, and Eldon J. Ullmer, The Florida State University*

Motivation—*Ivan L. Russell, University of Missouri— St. Louis*

Group Processes in the Classroom—*Richard A. Schmuck, University of Oregon, and Patricia A. Schmuck*

Encouraging Creativity in the Classroom—*E. Paul Torrance, University of Georgia*

classroom evaluation for teachers

Henry Dizney
University of Oregon

WM. C. BROWN COMPANY PUBLISHERS
Dubuque, Iowa

To Nancy and her progeny, who know the score.

Contents

List of Tables ....

List of Figures ....

Preface vii

1. Issues in Educational Evaluation 1

   The Purposes of Education 1
   Evaluation and Measurement 7
   Claims and Counterclaims in Perspective 10
   A Brief History 14

2. Foundations of Evaluation 25

   The Empirical View 26
   Educational Measurement 28
   Numbers and Scales 30

3. The Treatment of Empirical Data 37

   Description and Inference 37
   Frequency Distributions and Graphs 38
   Graphical Representation of Frequency Distributions 45
   Averages 53
   Ranks and Relative Ranks 58
   Variability 65
   Time to Solve an Arithmetic Problem 70
   Standard Scores 72
   Relationships 73

4. Instructional Assessment and Test Construction 82

   Educational Systems: The Classroom and Beyond 82
   Variables in Instruction 86
   Test Formats and Measurement 90

5. Validity and Reliability 97

   Standardized Tests 98
   Classroom Tests 104
   Concluding Comments 115

Index 117

List of Tables

1. Characteristics of Three Levels of Educational Objectives 6
2. Interrelationships and Definitions for Evaluation, Measurement, and Testing 8
3. Heights of Ten Children, Given to the Nearest Inch 38
4. Spelling Scores for a Group of 48 Pupils Organized into Three Alternative Frequency Distributions 40
5. Spelling Scores Organized as Grouped Frequency Distributions of Three Forms 43
6. Grouped Frequency Distribution Incorporating Cumulative Frequencies, Relative Frequencies, and Relative Cumulative Frequencies 45
7. General Types of Score Distributions, Their Characteristics and Possible "Cause" in Educational Situations 50
8. Distribution of Height Measures Illustrating Percentile Ranks 60
9. Percentile Ranks Determined for Spelling Score Distributions 61
10. Diagrammed, Step-by-Step Examples for Determining Percentiles by Interpolation 64
11. General Verbal Statements Suggesting the Strength of Association between Variables Represented by Various Values of r 76
12. Computational Illustration for Correlation Coefficient (r) 77
13. Computational Illustration of Rank Difference Coefficient of Correlation, Rho 79
14. Classes of Intellectual Behavior, Definitions, and Examples from Bloom's *Taxonomy of Educational Objectives* 88
15. Classes of Affective Behavior, Definitions, and Examples from Krathwohl's *Taxonomy of Educational Objectives* 89
16. Summary of Types of Reliability Coefficients, Their Procedures, Error Sources, and Representative Test Reliabilities..103
17. Illustrative Item Analysis Data for a Twenty-five Item Test 110
18. Illustration of Computation of a Reliability Coefficient by K-R 20 113

List of Figures

1. Reciprocal Relationships among the Three Major Instructional Elements 9
2. Diagram of the Process of Measurement, and Examples of Two Types of Scales 32
3. Comparison of Measurement Scales 35
4. Illustrations of Measuring Continuous Variables 41
5. General Model for Graphs 46
6. Illustrative Histograms, Frequency Polygon, and Ogive 47
7. Normal Curve, Its Percentile Equivalents and Related Test Scales 51
8. Illustration of Quartiles and an Ogive Differentiating PRK and P 63
9. The Relationship between Raw Scores and Deviation Scores 68
10. Model of an Instructional System with Parallel Teaching, Learning, and Evaluation Paths 83

Preface

There can be several reasons beyond the idiosyncrasies of the author for writing a book. After admitting to either a degree of egoism or a need for self-punishment, one must attend to the hoped for relationship between the reader and the book. One possibility is that something inventive and important requires the attention of a given readership. The field of educational evaluation has had its share of creative personalities and, where lacking, has borrowed the ideas and wisdom of others from related fields. This book provides nothing new in terms of either the theory or the practice of educational evaluation. Its claim for attention must rather be based upon the need for written material that organizes important principles and concepts of measurement and evaluation for those who would use them. The book is, therefore, an aid to learning and understanding designed for the use of teachers and students of education.

Specifically, the book is aimed at students in either a first course in educational measurement or in a methods course which incorporates a fair degree of measurement and evaluation. Further, those teachers who are involved in instruction and feel the need for advancing their grasp of evaluation may find it helpful. Based upon the author's familiarity with both groups and his experience in teaching educational measurement and evaluation, the book evolved in certain unique ways.

The first chapter is an attempt to justify and place in context the processes of evaluation and measurement. The chapter is largely descriptive. The second chapter deals with the subject on the basis of principles and concepts in the belief that when such are understood, most procedural and technical problems are simplified. The third chapter is by and large devoted to skill-building in those techniques deemed essential to the practice of measurement. The fourth chapter provides further information important for test construction in its educational context. Chapter 5 is devoted to the fundamental concepts of reliability and validity, firstly from a constitutive, and secondly from an operational point-of-view. The purpose of the book, then, is to provide a useful discussion of educational evaluation for the development of both an understanding of its issues and some command of its procedures.

To achieve these ends, material which at first glance may seem to be too theoretical or somewhat unrelated is given. Wherever possible, this material has been "tied down" by example and illustration. Further, the book is heavily laced with tables, figures, displays, and examples. No formula or procedure is left unillustrated. Hopefully, these techniques will prove sufficient to ease the early steps of the typical student. In the final analysis, most of the quality of all education is in his hands.

Credits and appreciation are due to a number of people, some of whom have been obscured by time and in memory. I owe an abiding debt to many former teachers and professors for both their inspiration and skill. The Iowa group especially stands out in my mind as having been professionally devoted and able. My colleagues at Kent State and at the University of Oregon are valued sources of information and motivation. I especially wish to thank Dr. Arthur Mittman for his leadership and help; Dr. Kaoru Yamamoto for his support and encouragement; and Dr. James B. Stroud for his inspiration. I hope that, to all of these people and to my profession in general, my omissions are justifiable and my commissions tolerable. A number of students, past and present, have helped in countless ways. Their problems, behavior, and insights have provided for more learning than their instructor could absorb. They have acted as though they understood. The preparation of this book itself has been greatly aided by Sheelagh Bull, Joseph Bentley, and Gary Simonsen. I appreciate their critical comments and sound advice. Finally, I extend gratitude to two typist-confessors of exceptional skill, Mrs. Diane Waxler and Mrs. Carol Johnson, for their effort and ability.

H.D.

1

Issues in
Educational Evaluation

Education in the United States is a vast enterprise. Recent statistics indicate that school enrollments include approximately 37 million elementary pupils, 14 million secondary pupils, and 6.7 million college students.[1] These students are enrolled in roughly 125,000 schools, colleges, and universities. In the public schools alone, some 965,000 elementary and 735,000 secondary teachers are engaged in instruction. Again only in the public school sector, about 39 billion dollars were spent directly for education in 1968-69. All projections of these data suggest a quickening and intensification of effort in the immediate future. These statistics are, of course, only part of the story. They do not directly tell of the more important aspects of education, such as its significance to individuals and to society. These more fundamental though complex results represent instructional outcomes. It is clear that, as more and more students enter the classrooms each year, new demands will be made upon the educational system. We will not only teach more students, but we will be required to teach them more effectively. This being the case, it is in the teacher's self-interest to understand fully the process and improvement of instruction. Such understanding cannot be achieved without a knowledge of evaluation.

The Purposes of Education

An understanding of educational evaluation can best be achieved by first considering the general process of education. For this reason, we shall attempt to "place" the process of educational evaluation in its proper context.

---

[1]U.S. Office of Education, *Digest of Educational Statistics,* 1968 Edition (Washington, D.C.: U.S. Government Printing Office, 1968).

An interesting pamphlet[2] written for persons not acquainted with American education states that the broad purposes of education in the United States are:

1. The development of the individual;
2. The achievement of the maximum welfare of society through the cooperative efforts of individuals and groups.

These statements seem simple and straightforward. But, like statements of purpose for homes, churches, and governments, they are deceptive. The fact that we are inclined to read and immediately accept them may mean: (1) that they are "true" and therefore should be accepted; or (2) that we have not thought about them sufficiently. It is probably true that, in any endeavor, statements of purpose are useful. At the very least, it is characteristic of institutions to provide such statements. The efficiency and robustness of the endeavor can frequently be assessed by the degree of agreement between institutional claims and achievement. Education is no exception. It requires and does provide its *raison d'etre*. This fundamentally provides the beginning reference for all that is undertaken by the enterprise. It is, in large measure, a matter of practice whether or not the purposes are fulfilled. The first purpose of educational evaluation, then, is to consider this very problem, namely, the degree to which its purposes are met.

Important Terms

Let us introduce some educational terminology so that we may more effectively deal with evaluation's place in education. The previously stated purposes are commonly called goals or general objectives. They are just that. They state the ultimate outcomes of education in the most general possible way. They justify and orient. Unfortunately, they do not specify. They require explication in order to be useful at the level of instruction and evaluation. The problem is to translate such goals into workable statements of purpose that will be useful in instructional planning. To do this requires roughly two steps. Firstly, what we may call intermediate objectives need to be derived. Intermediate objectives are statements of purpose appropriate to a more specific educational level or context, (e.g., the first grade or junior high school, mathematics or physical education, etc.). Secondly, the intermediate objectives need further to be distilled into what are called immediate or specific instructional objectives. Examples of specific objectives might be: (1) pupil can combine quantities accurately; or (2) pupil can formulate complete sentences. This class of objectives specifies, insofar as possible, purposes

---

[2]U.S. Department of Health, Education, and Welfare, *Education in the United States of America* (Washington, D.C.: U.S. Government Printing Office, 1960).

of instruction in units of behavior and content at a level specific enough to indicate procedures (educational experience) and results (learning). More will be said about specific objectives in Chapter 4.

Ultimate Objectives

At this point, it is sufficient to recognize certain characteristics of ultimate educational objectives and, by implication, education itself. In the United States, education is compulsory first, and selective second. One is tempted to suggest that its monopolistic character is one explanation for what educators consider its great demand. The compulsory character of public education influences the kinds of ultimate objectives given to it. It is obvious that these objectives will either reflect those purposes deemed so essential that they justify the compulsion, or they will be so elastic as to cover all contingencies. Perhaps, the educational goals given earlier illustrate both points. It is assumed that both "individual development" and "welfare of society" are universally valid. It is also apparent that neither specifies much. You and I will argue only when we begin to translate into specifics what these purposes mean in terms of student behavior and how these ends can best be achieved. To undertake that process, the translator will have to consider systems of value, as well as knowledge, methods of instruction, theories of learning, and characteristics of learners. This requirement should lead to caution on the part of educators and critics alike, and it precludes the use of quick and ready schemes for the salvation of public instruction (see the next available Sunday supplement for an illustration of this point).

As has been suggested, general educational objectives state the ultimate purposes of education in the broadest possible terms. The strength of such statements is that they are thus generally applicable to diverse programs and groups. The weakness of such statements is that they do not specify. They do not guide either instruction or pupils in specific ways. One of the assumptions of modern education is that broad statements like "the development of the individual" can be stated in terms of behavior of the individual. This position is consistent with scientific empiricism and stems from the school of *behaviorism* in psychology. This school of thought goes even further, maintaining that we can only know "what's going on" regarding individuals in terms of their behavior and/or changes in their behavior. Such an assumption provides for utilizing objective evidence instead of subjective judgment in the study and understanding of human beings and other living acting things (like white rats). Granting this assumption, our ultimate objectives will become meaningful only insofar as we are able to specify the behaviors they suggest. One means of doing this is to deal with broad classes of behavior such as intellectual, emotional, physical, or social behaviors. Currently, there are several excellent "taxonomies" of educational objectives which have dealt with the behavior of education in the areas of cognitive, affective, and psychomotor behaviors.[3] No doubt others will be developed and added as our understanding of human behavior and education expand.

To refer back to the ultimate objectives being used for illustrative purposes, namely, "development of the individual" and "welfare of society," we may, on the basis of additional assumptions, be able to begin to specify what we mean by individual development and social welfare in terms of behaviors leading to them. Such behaviors may be intellectual, emotional, physical, or social, or combinations of behaviors from all four classes. At this point, we may well conclude that education as experienced in schools can meet certain of these objectives but not others. Indeed, schools have been criticized for attempting too much in terms of their objectives or for attempting to meet objectives better achieved by other institutions. For example, schools have been criticized for undertaking objectives in the areas of ethics and morality. Interestingly, they have also been criticized for *not* doing so which, perhaps, illustrates the importance of judgment and values when general educational objectives are considered.

Intermediate Objectives

Intermediate educational objectives represent an effort to begin the delineation and specification of general educational objectives. They imply in fairly broad terms what is to be done toward achieving the general objectives. As such, they are not as specific as is eventually necessary to guide and evaluate educational experiences explicitly, but rather, they represent transitional statements between ultimate purposes and specific behaviors. They are necessary for the referencing of both blocks of educational experience and the several disciplines. That is, they state objectives appropriate to grade levels or to administrative units and/or fields of study such as mathematics, language arts, and physical education. Intermediate objectives usually represent an assumed relationship to general objectives and may be considered to have been derived logically from them. Typically, they are developed by curriculum committees, state departments of education, or authoritative groups such as the Commission on Science Education from the American Asso-

---

[3]B. S. Bloom, ed., *Taxonomy of Educational Objectives. Handbook I: Cognitive Domain* (New York: David McKay Co., 1956).

D. R. Krathwohl, B. S. Bloom, and B. B. Masia, *Taxonomy of Educational Objectives: The Classification of Educational Goals. Handbook II: Affective Domain* (New York: David McKay Co., 1964).

ciation for the Advancement of Science. As has been suggested, whether or not intermediate objectives are logically consistent with general objectives and from whatever source they are available, functionally they represent transitional statements tying specific objectives and ultimate purposes together. Some examples may be useful. The New York City School's *Grade Guide*: 5-6[4] states the objectives for the elementary school in mathematics as:

1. To develop mathematical concepts, and understandings of relationships among measures, numbers, and processes.
2. To develop mastery of basic number facts and techniques of computation.
3. To use mathematical knowledge and computational skill in solving problems.
4. To develop interest and assurance in using mathematics for the purpose of solving problems in children's experiences.

An excellent example of intermediate objectives is available in the recently developed science materials and program of the American Association for the Advancement of Science.[5] Although they are not identified as intermediate objectives in their source, they are transitional statements bridging ultimate purposes and specific behavioral objectives. They are, in paraphrased form,[6] development by the student of abilities in:

1. stating problems
2. utilizing sources of reliable information
3. making observations
4. comparing phenomena
5. building systems of classification
6. using scientific instruments
7. using processes of measurement
8. devising experiments
9. evaluating evidence and drawing conclusions
10. inventing models and theories

Few would argue that each of the examples of intermediate objectives just given could not be assumed to be related either to the "development of the individual" or to the "welfare of society." What is arguable, perhaps, is whether or not they represent the best or most efficient of many possibilities. Their derivation and choice, it would seem, remain in American education a matter of constant effort and revision. Frequently, they will represent the voice of authority of groups concerned with

---

[4]Reprinted from *Grade Guide*: 5-6 by permission of the Board of Education of the City of New York. (New York: Publications Sales Office, 1962).

[5]Commission on Science Education, *Science—A Process Approach, Commentary for Teachers*, 3d experimental edition. (Washington, D.C.: American Association for the Advancement of Science, 1968).

[6]Ibid., pp. 2-3.

curricular matters. It would be unwise to ignore such authority and its implied experience. Sometimes these objectives will represent pressure by various groups interested in the conduct of education. This would seem inescapable in a democracy, and again, it would be foolish to ignore such pressure. It would be equally foolish to perceive such objectives as dogma to be followed without the exercise of judgment.

Specific Instructional Objectives

One more step remains, namely, the derivation of specific instructional objectives. Here the teacher will find both the challenge and the responsibility of operationalizing the foregoing objectives into statements so specific that they virtually guide instruction and define evaluation. To many, this is the heart of teaching and the foundation of evaluation. In Chapter 4, we will consider specific objectives more fully.

Table 1 is a presentation of what have been referred to in this discussion as general, intermediate, and specific objectives in education

TABLE 1

Characteristics of Three Levels of Educational Objectives

Level of Objective:	General (Ultimate)	→ Intermediate (Transitional)	→ Specific (Terminal)
Source:	Society itself; represents values	Curricular Groups, State or School System or Special Committee representing discipline or educational levels: In part derived from Ultimate objectives.	Derived from Intermediate Objective by teacher, instructor, or other personnel directly related to specific instruction.
Purpose:	To orient and set general purpose	To delineate and translate values of general objectives to more specific statements of content and behavior.	To specify behavior, guide instruction and evaluation directly.
Target:	The total educational system and ultimate outcomes	Blocks of education such as grade groupings or disciplines such as science, art, etc.	The individual learner and collective groups of learners.
Example:	The development of the individual	To develop mathematical concepts and understandings of relationships among measures, numbers, and processes.	The student can accurately determine the surface area of physical objects. The student can convert temperature from F to C scales.

and some of their characteristics. Not all educators would agree completely with the terminology or the details of this presentation. The same would be true of personnel in measurement and evaluation. All would agree, however, that objectives are essential to both instruction and its evaluation. Further, they would agree that objectives are complex, that they represent multiple influences, and that they are subject to continual critical review and revision.

Evaluation and Measurement

As in other aspects of education, there are terminological problems in evaluation. Such problems are not solely matters of definition, but they also reflect usage, custom, and the tendency to deal imprecisely with meanings. One seemingly common problem is an unnecessarily narrow view that equates testing, measurement, and evaluation. Characteristic of this view are beliefs that acts and procedures are equivalent to purposes and processes: for example, that a test or test-taking is synonomous with evaluation; or that the only way to measure the attainment of an educational objective is by use of a paper-pencil test, preferably machine-scored and ideally saturated with the jargon of measurement. Such views suggest confusion and misunderstanding at a quite fundamental level.

Testing and Measurement

Noll[7] has dealt with the confusion in usage between testing, measurement, and evaluation. Roughly, we may say testing deals with the use of tests and emphasizes the instrument, as it were. Measurement is a process. It has been defined as "the process of assigning numerals to objects according to rules."[8] More will be said about this definition in Chapter 2. For the present, let us simply consider measurement to be a process which results in a set of symbols representing selected characteristics of things in which we are interested. Various functions such as classification, comparison, ranking, description of status or change, and prediction are all implied by this definition. Different techniques or instruments may be utilized to fulfill these functions. For example, one might consider not only the use of several kinds of tests to measure achievement, but also other kinds of systematic observation such as rating scales, score cards, or characteristics of concrete products. It has often been suggested that measurement refers to quantity, that is,

---

[7]Victor H. Noll, *Introduction to Educational Measurement*. (Boston: Houghton Mifflin Co., 1957).

[8]S. S. Stevens, "Mathematics, Measurement, and Psychophysics," in *Handbook of Experimental Psychology*, ed. S. S. Stevens (New York: John Wiley & Sons, 1951), Ch. 1, p. 1.

questions of how much. In a sense, this is so, but the choice of characteristics to be quantified and the nature of the symbolic system used
qualify that usage. Questions of *how much* in educational measurement
are rarely, if ever, simple or obvious.

Evaluation

Compared to measurement, the process of evaluation is even more
complex. It has commonly been said that evaluation deals with value
and quality. This suggests questions and judgments of worth rather
than amount, (e.g., How good is this? vs. How much is this?). Or it
suggests a qualitative process as opposed to the quantitative process of
measurement. Further, evaluation suggests a more inclusive process
than measurement, a process which incorporates quantitative statements
en route to value judgments. This usage would seem to promise great
relevance in education. If we think again of the general purposes of
education, we find it is clear that they require a process for making
value judgments about phenomena in terms of procedures designed for
making observations. Thus, evaluation, measurement, and testing. The
trilogy is interdependent, with each facet interacting with all others.
An appreciation and understanding of these interactions is an interesting and challenging aspect of education. Table 2 summarizes the given
definitions and interrelationships.

One of the dangers of dealing at the conceptual level with evaluation
as a process in education is that the complexity of the contexts in which
it occurs is likely to be oversimplified. A way to deal with this is to
consider the major factors in instruction and to suggest some of the
variables at work. Conceptualizations of educational programming frequently suggest that there are three major elements in the teaching-

TABLE 2

Interrelationships and Definitions for Evaluation, Measurement, and Testing

Term	Definition	Key Synonym or Synonymous Concept	Reference Points
Evaluation	A process of determin- ing worth or for inter- preting information from	Judgment of merit	Educational goals, pur- poses, objectives
Measurement	a process for gaining a symbolic system to re- present characteristics obtained by	Symbolic represen- tation	Trait, characteristics, be havior
Testing	procedures for systema- tizing observations.	Instruments	Tests, rating scales, ob- servation schedules.

learning process. They are the determination of objectives, the planning and organization of experiences and materials for fulfilling the objectives, and the evaluation of the educational program. Figure 1 is an adaptation of a figure presented by Furst[9] to schematize the reciprocal relations among these elements. On the face of it, Figure 1 suggests interplaying influences among the major elements. Part of the interplay is a result of redundance or commonness among the elements, (e.g., each deals with learner behavior). Also, part of the interplay is built into the system as corrective feedback, (e.g., curriculum may be changed or adapted to suit a given objective as a result of evaluative information, etc.). Some of

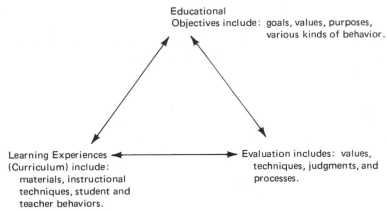

Educational
Objectives include: goals, values, purposes,
various kinds of behavior.

Learning Experiences
(Curriculum) include:
    materials, instructional
    techniques, student and
    teacher behaviors.

Evaluation includes: values,
    techniques, judgments, and
    processes.

*From *Constructing Evaluation Instruments* by E. J. Furst (New York: Longmans, Green & Co., 1958). An adaptation, reprinted by permission of David McKay Co., Inc.

Figure 1. Reciprocal Relationships among the Three Major Instructional Elements.

the variables affecting the elements of the system are cultural values, political pressure, historical precedent, cost and availability of materials, characteristics of learners and teachers (ability, interest, perceptions, temperament, etc.), school plant, budget, quality of measurement, astuteness of evaluation, ad infinitum. To think of evaluation or curriculum or objectives as the key to control and success of the system is to miss the essence of education. It is vastly complex and resistant. A better grasp of evaluation will help in the understanding of the system and will result in its improvement. For the teacher, it is, perhaps, sufficient to recognize and appreciate the opportunities and limitations within the complexities.

[9] E. J. Furst, *Constructing Evaluation Instruments* (New York: Longmans, Green & Co., 1958), p. 3.

It should be apparent from this discussion that evaluation can serve several purposes in education. It can be useful in the formulation and modification of both objectives and instructional procedures, thus functioning as a feedback mechanism. Given objectives are formulated, leading to instructional planning and implementation. The resulting learning is then evaluated, and this may lead to modification or confirmation of either or both. Further, evaluation may reveal limitations in evaluation procedures themselves. Many of the techniques and concepts that we shall consider are designed specifically for this purpose. In addition, evaluation provides information directly useful to learners for several purposes. Because it can provide information leading to improved descriptions of those traits (notably achievement) that are important in education, this information may be used to meet more successfully the educational needs and purposes of the learner. It is, on the same basis, useful to classroom teachers. Improved group and individual programming should be the result.

Claims and Counterclaims in Perspective

Psychometricians and measurement specialists have been among the proponents of systematic evaluation in education. Their influence has been great and may be seen in many ways. Grades and grade point averages, standardized achievement tests, intelligence tests, personality tests, anecdotal and cumulative records, proficiency tests, programmed instruction, required tests and measurement courses for teacher trainees, measurement conferences and workshops, and many other aspects of American education attest to the influence of their point of view. On the other hand, an articulate body of critics of measurement (and of certain methods of evaluation by implication) have been increasingly presenting their case to educators and to the general public. It is worth the time to consider briefly the extremes of this controversy, to try to understand it, and to settle upon some position.

"Whatever Exists . . . ."

Perhaps the position stated by Thorndike more than fifty years ago summarizes one extreme in the measurement controversy. He said: "Whatever exists at all exists in some amount."[10] Others have appended: ". . . and can be measured." Of course, Thorndike said a great deal more and was fully aware of difficulties in "mental measurement." For example, he explicitly mentioned as special difficulties in measuring

---

[10]E. L. Thorndike, "The Nature, Purposes and General Methods of Measurements of Educational Products," *The Measurement of Educational Products.* 17th Yearbook of the National Society for the Study of Education, 1918, Part II.

human behavior (1) the absence or imperfection of units of measurement, (2) lack of constancy in things measured, and (3) the extreme complexity of the measurements desired.[11] It is interesting that many of the critics of measurement and evaluation use these same difficulties as points in their argument. Also, it is to be expected, since these weaknesses are valid and telling limitations to some of the measurement practices of today.

Unlike Thorndike, there are proponents in the measurement movement in education who do not temper their position by considering limitations. To these extremists, the notion that "if anything exists, it exists in some amount and is measurable" can be turned around to state that "any available measure represents a meaningful trait by definition and its use justifies its existence." It is not unknown that educational measures are used for prediction and selection in the face of very marginal validity evidence. The best known and respected test publishers in this country offer tests which are misused, or worse, for which there is no clear use. Unlike medicine, tests are generally available to users with little if any evidence regarding the qualifications of the user. In spite of this, test proponents sometimes argue that tests can be utilized for prediction and selection, and that, therefore, an open market in test instruments is desirable. Occasionally, professional organizations issue statements regarding test ethics and standards, but, by and large, such statements are unenforced and unenforceable. One of the writer's colleagues frequently states after students have been selected for graduate training in his department (and, incidentally, after others have been rejected) "Science triumphs again!" This comment suggests a certain uneasiness all the way around in the ability of our criteria for admission to be rigorously defended. And yet we continue to apply them with less than a fully critical attitude relying on the usual reasons of need, convenience, and custom. Is it any wonder that reasonable critics look askance at such practice?

These same critics would be justified in finding fault with those who insist that the only respectable procedures for operationalizing instruction and learning involves a formal record. To these enthusiasts, test scores or counts or tallies obtained under "standardized" conditions constitute the definition of learning. Consequently, a test score is considered to be direct and complete evidence of learning. That such measures can be considered estimates and that error in such estimates arises in part from the imperfections of the measures themselves under this view is disallowed. This position usually considers validity in a narrow

---

[11]E. L. Thorndike, *Mental and Social Measurements*. (New York: Teachers College Press, Teachers College, Columbia University, 1919).

context of fairly immediate contingencies and often substitutes technical reliability for evidence of relevance. It is an extremely pragmatic and data-centered frame of reference.

Cult of Efficiency

Another extreme among the proponents is to argue from the complexity of education and the need for efficiency in view of the always limited resources. Since public education is charged with providing service to overwhelmingly large groups with multiple and complex purposes, and since it has limited resources, necessity dictates the use of measurement procedures to aid in making educational decisions. Such decisions include selection, differentiation, remediation, and the provision of data for self-initiated choice making. We measure because we must. Under these conditions, it is all too easy for the *purpose* of measurement to be altered so that the availability of measurement data leads to a decision by formula in an oversimplified reduction of the process of decision making.

Testing and Motivation

Finally, there are other proponents who claim great motivational and learning benefits from educational measurement. Tests can, of course, be challenging and educationally rewarding. They can also be deadening influences upon student behavior. Enthusiastic supporters of measurement in education would do well to consider that tests are not automatically either beneficial or harmful. Apart from criticisms based on the inherent difficulties in measurement pointed out by Thorndike, the extreme views of some measurement proponents create further grounds on which to base criticism. Naturally, critics of measurement have risen to these challenges. In addition, though, a number of critics of the testing movement and measurement practices have given voice to what would seem to be a natural distrust of measurement and evaluation in our culture. It is possible that suspicion, if not antagonism, toward educational evaluation has its roots in the ideals of democracy and the tradition of individualism. Our culture seems to have idealized achievement "against the odds" and the unpredicted event. Underdogs are essentially poor bets in the predictive sense. Our empathy for them suggests that there is natural sympathy for and identification with the individual who can overcome the usual contingencies. We even laud the winner in chance events such as raffles and sweepstakes. If this is the case, one may expect the serious critic—and serious critics there are—to play to full houses. They may verbalize what we want to believe. They may also provide much needed correctives for misuse and abuse.

Some Critics' Views

Several years ago, a committee on testing was established by three important national educational groups. The committee wrote an interesting pamphlet entitled *Testing Testing Testing*.[12] Its purpose was neither to condemn nor to praise the use of tests, but rather to assess impartially the impact of testing upon the American educational scene. The report restricted itself to the impact upon education of what were called "external" tests, by which the committee meant commercially available and professionally developed tests. A number of important evaluative issues were raised that suggest a host of problems in testing and evaluation practices. The general tone of the report was critical. Specifically, it charged that test data are incomplete, subject to misinterpretation, expensive in time and money, lead to oversimplification, and unduly influence curricular content. To deny these charges as being either misguided or uninformed would be foolish. To accept them at face value would be equally foolish.

Similarly, we should consider carefully the criticisms against testing leveled by critics appealing to the general public. One such critic, Hoffmann,[13] has, by the identification of particular test items in specific tests, charged that bright and creative students are penalized by test practices. He argues that multiple-choice tests especially reward superficial learners who are more adept at storing factual and stereotyped information than in conceiving or solving problems of more general significance. Beyond this, Hoffman implies that the effects of tests in general have serious and negative influences upon the national interest. Wernick[14] maintains that we live in a test-plagued society controlled to some extent by the psychometrician. He suggests that the whole basis for employing tests is so shaky that tactics such as cheating and physical refusal to be tested are justifiable on the part of examinees. A less radical position is held by Huff,[15] but its purpose is similar in that he maintains that tests are a necessary but distasteful reality to which test takers must adapt. Short of cheating, the adaptive process as used by Huff is called "testmanship." It consists of tricks of the trade in the form of tips designed to provide an edge for the informed. It would seem that larceny

---

[12]Joint Committee on Testing. *Testing Testing Testing*. (Washington, D.C.: American Association of School Administrators, Council of Chief State School Officers, National Association of Secondary School Principals. 1962).

[13]Banesh Hoffmann, *The Tyranny of Testing* (New York: Crowell, Collier & Macmillan, 1962).

[14]Robert Wernick, *They've Got Your Number* (New York: W. W. Norton & Co., 1956).

[15]Darrell Huff, *Score: The Strategy of Taking Tests* (New York: Ballantine Books, 1961).

which generalizes is more tolerable than straight theft. Ballinger,[16] in a more traditional sense, supports the notion that tests have flaws, that examinees are differentially prepared for the process of test taking, and more seriously, that a national investigation into the impact of testing upon people's lives should be undertaken.

Evaluation in Perspective

And so we come to the point where the claims and counterclaims of the extremists beg resolution. Are tests inherently good or bad? Is measurement either so fundamentally appropriate or inappropriate to education that it should be, must be, totally accepted or abandoned? Is evaluation essential to instruction? A perspective with respect to these questions is in order.

It would be well first to establish that the extremists, either pro or con regarding measurement and evaluation, are few in number. It is alleged, but difficult to confirm, that there are measurement critics who are so extreme that they maintain measurement and evaluation should be abandoned because of its consequences. Most educators and measurement experts alike view evaluation in a broader context. They see the limitations as well as the usefulness of evaluative procedures. Of course, there are weak test items, poorly constructed tests, and inappropriate educational practices stemming from them. Misuse and misunderstanding of evaluative data is not uncommon. But are these sufficient arguments for discontinuing tests, measurement procedures, and the process of evaluation? Most educators would answer no, for to reply in the affirmative leads one to even more severe criticism and crippling positions. Imagine an evaluation-free educational system if you can. Think of instruction as it would proceed without measurement. That path would lead to educational anarchy. We do, however, wish to be as critical of malpractice as possible. The rest of this book is devoted to establishing that very attitude. The rest of your professional life should include the same objective. There is much to be gained for the teacher from the serious study of evaluation, but before we can intelligently critique the process, we must understand its limitations. In that direction lies improvement and effectiveness.

A Brief History

Evaluation, measurement, and testing have a long history in human affairs. Wherever man has judged, observed, or performed, he has engaged in these processes. Greek history establishes that, in ancient times,

---

[16]Stanley E. Ballinger, "Of Testing and Its Tyranny," *Phi Delta Kappan*, XLIV, (Jan. 1963), pp. 176-180.

these processes were associated with the education and training of the young. Biblical reference and early Chinese recorded history indicate the same thing. Anthropological studies of primitive cultures commonly refer to tests of maturity and knowledge and suggest them as inherent pieces of the fabric of culture. Whether ancient or modern, domestic or foreign, apparently youth is always subject not only to instruction and training, but inescapably also to assessment and evaluation. As Chauncey and Dobbin[17] have said, the intellectual testing of the young by the early Greeks was closely associated with teaching. The so-called Socratic method of instruction, with emphasis upon the leading question and the importance of the response, illustrates this. The evolution of our contemporary evaluation practices in an historical frame of reference is a fascinating study in itself. We shall briefly consider that history and its meaning in contemporary educational evaluation.

The systematic measurement and evaluation of educational achievement is surprisingly recent, if we take as a requirement *standardized* procedures. Standardized procedures as used here will mean pre-established tasks, common to a set of examinees, with the possibility for inter-examinee comparisons. This definition is worth some discussion.

If one chooses to measure children's growth for evaluative purposes, the measures employed will not be useful unless the procedures for obtaining them are comparable. If the evaluator reports different aspects of children's growth, no matter how accurately, the evaluation will suffer. One child's teeth status cannot be compared to another's height and a third's weight. Given the same aspect of growth to evaluate, we will still insist upon further standardization. If we wish to evaluate height, we will require comparable procedures for obtaining that evaluation. We would not consider distance from top of head to ceiling in units of book thickness as useful. We would impose rules to gain comparability such as shoes off, stand straight, align the ruler from the floor, record in comparable units.

In a test to be used for evaluation, we must know (control) what was required in the performance, under established conditions, and have a basis for judging the result. It is not solely convention that dictates that running events in a track meet proceed from a common start over the same course to one finish line. Imagine the result if the mile run were conducted from the center of a circle with a one mile radius and all runners choosing whatever direction personal factors suggested! It might be an interesting event, but would it be standardized?

The point of the preceding discussion is to provide some understanding of necessary conditions for educational measurement—past and

---

[17]Henry Chauncey and J. E. Dobbin, *Testing: Its Place in Education Today.* (New York: Harper & Row, 1963).

present. Problems of standardization were appreciated by our educational forefathers. Their solution was neither instantaneous nor easy and, in fact, we are still searching to improve educational measurement today. In practice, some of the assumptions of the modern psychometrician are not met. For example, in educational measurement, do all children in a group start from a common point? Do they all perform with their best effort? Are extraneous factors to the evaluation, which influence the result, equally distributed among examinees? The answers to these questions are obvious. Psychometricians have methods for dealing with the measurement problems they raise, but the qualifications in evaluation which are suggested are not well understood by teachers.

Historically, there are three major sources which we may pursue toward understanding present evaluative practices. They come from the histories of achievement testing (education), mental and clinical testing (psychology), and statistics (psychometrics, in this case).

Educational Testing

As has been suggested, measurement and evaluation have long been associated with instruction. Historically, they were informal, give and take processes intertwined with the teacher's procedures and the student's learning. That is precisely where they should have been—if one could have depended upon them. The difficulty was that such measurement was frequently biased, often capricious, and usually arbitrary. At an early date in American public education, students were examined, usually orally, either by members of boards of education or by their representatives. The purpose of such examinations was to demonstrate competency, and the practice was probably imported from Europe. In 1845, Horace Mann introduced uniform written examinations in place of oral examinations of pupils in the Boston public schools. According to Chauncey and Dobbin,[18] Mann claimed that the advantages of his testing innovation included greater impartiality, control of examiner interference, uniformity of questions reducing the influence of chance in terms of their difficulty, conservation of examiner time, wider sampling of content, and uniform conditions. These conclusions on the part of Mann indicate a general awareness of limitations in the oral examination procedures of his day. They are also startlingly like the problems with which modern evaluators contend.

Perhaps the first truly standardized tests used in educational research were developed by Joseph M. Rice in 1897.[19] Rice, a physician, was in-

---

[18]Ibid., p. 11.

[19]J. M. Rice, *The Rational Spelling Book* (New York, Cincinnati: American Book Co., 1898).

terested in a school controversy of the day over the question of "liberalizing" the curriculum. The "establishment" maintained that there was not enough time in school to achieve all the things it was already charged with, let alone to add innovations. Rice hit upon the expediency of empiricism to resolve the issue. He developed a fifty-word spelling test and administered it to school children in towns where he happened to be from time to time. More importantly, he kept accurate records of the pupils' spelling performance and developed what were essentially achievement norms. He found, to the amazement of the "dataless" establishment, that spelling achievement was largely independent of instructional time spent on spelling. You would probably not be satisfied with Rice's data to resolve the curricular issue because you have grown up with scientific inquiry. But at that time, it was truly a great stroke for both educational measurement and empiricism. Others quickly grasped the significance of Rice's work.

Developed during that period were two wide-scale standardized achievement test programs that survive today. The New York State Regents Examinations were founded during the years 1865-1878, and the College Entrance Examination Board was established in the year 1900.[20] They were not, of course, standardized tests as we know them today, but they were uniform, and in revised form, they are active and influential in education today.

Shortly after these beginnings of standardized tests, Professor E. L. Thorndike of Columbia University published, in 1904, the first textbook on educational measurement.[21] In that decade and in succeeding ones, a wide range of standardized tests was written. Stone developed an arithmetic reasoning ability test in 1908; Courtis, a test of arithmetic computation in 1909. Thorndike published a handwriting scale for the evaluation of that skill in 1910. Ayres' handwriting scale came in 1912; Hillegas' scale for English compositions in 1912; Buckingham's spelling power test in 1913; Thorndike's vocabulary test in 1914, followed by 1915 and 1916 improved versions; Starch, in the same years, contributed reading, English grammar, and Latin vocabulary tests, and there were others.

By the 1920's, achievement batteries were introduced. The first, the *Stanford Achievement Test,* appeared in 1923 and was developed under the authorship of L. M. Terman, T. L. Kelly, and G. M. Reech. Today there are many such batteries available. Among the ones most commonly used are the *Iowa Tests of Basic Skills,* the *California Achievement Tests,*

---

[20]J. E. Horrocks and Thelma A. Schoonover, *Measurement for Teachers* (Columbus: Charles E. Merrill Publishing Co., 1968).
[21]E. L. Thorndike, *An Introduction to the Theory of Mental and Social Measurement* (New York: Teachers College Press, Teachers College, Columbia University, 1904, rev. ed. 1913).

the *Metropolitan Achievement Battery,* and the *Stanford Achievement Test.* Other comparable batteries are available for high school students, including the *Iowa Tests of Educational Development, Sequential Tests of Educational Progress,* and *School and College Ability Tests.* Each of these batteries follows the lead of the *Stanford Achievement Test* and incorporates improvements over other earlier tests. They are professionally developed by teams of experts and are underwritten by large publishing firms which can systematically sample the objectives of the curriculum in a way that no one person could. Further, the capital of the publisher allows field testing, tryout, revision, and norm development *before* sale that one pocket could never afford. Also, major educational test publishers assume the responsibility of demonstrating the quality of their merchandise. They scientifically undertake the technical tasks of estimating the various reliabilities and validities essential to the consumer. Test publishers also develop and standardize intelligence tests for groups and individuals. The historical development of these intelligence tests is discussed in the following section.

Psychological Testing

Of the many attributes of human behavior in psychological testing, probably intelligence enjoys the best known historical record. Human characteristics, especially physical characteristics, have been measured since ancient times. Likewise, human performance, especially physical performance as in athletic contests or tests of endurance and strength, have also been measured.

It is surprising, in the light of these precedents, just how recent is the practice of measuring man's mental, emotional, and personality characteristics. Psychologists date the measurement of man's pyschological behavior from the year 1879. It was during that year that Wundt established a psychological laboratory in Leipzig and began recording human reaction time to and perception of sensory stimuli. This was a bold effort in that phenomena not directly observable were made the subject of scientific inquiry.

Against this background, a most predictable sort of pressure was brought to bear upon psychologists. The problem that precipitated the pressure was, in its broadest sense, a social one. Specifically, educators and others had for years been trying to improve the plight of the mentally retarded. Segregation and special training seemed to be the logical answers. But, of course, the segregation of slow learners, or anyone else, presupposes their identifiability. Therefore, the problem presented to the new discipline of psychology was to devise procedures for the identification of those who were genuinely mentally handicapped. Such procedures would need to make distinctions between those who were indolent, those who chose not to achieve, the quiet achiever, and other classes of school "failure," as well as the target group, those with limited capacity to learn.

As one might expect, psychologists first began by seeking relationships (correlates) between physical characteristics and mental ability. Size of skull, reaction time to stimuli, efficiency of sensory mechanisms, general appearance, and so forth were all tried as potential indices of intelligence. None proved effective because gross physical characteristics simply do not differentiate mental abilities, as any female blond can tell us. This kind of effort is of interest, however, as it was the foundation of a number of pseudopsychological sciences. Among these were phenology, somato-typologies, and others that variously indicate that we should expect happiness from fat folks, lack of character in people with recessive chins, and the like. Palmistry, judging character by means of studying a person's handwriting or his facial profile, and many other divining techniques have all proven fruitless when put to the test. This is an important lesson to be learned from and about all psychological tests, that is, a test or procedure is only as good as its validity indicates. In other words, the test or technique must demonstrate its meaningfulness and utility with objective and acceptable evidence.

In 1904, the Paris school authorities commissioned Alfred Binet and others to devise methods for identifying mentally retarded children.[22] Apparently, Binet had had experience in the quest for simple physical correlates of mental ability. From this experience and his own wisdom as a psychologist, he theorized about the way that mental ability manifests itself. If he could accurately theorize, it was obvious that he would be in an improved position for achieving the task at hand. Binet further felt, and no one has disputed his reasoning as yet, that intelligence was not subject to direct observation, but that it could only be inferred indirectly in the behavior of individuals. These are important points to remember about scientific research: (1) the odds always favor the investigator using the weight of logic and theory, and (2) complex phenomena frequently require indirect measurement. Classroom teachers would do well to recognize these points in dealing with the complexities of classroom learning.

From this base, Binet concluded that intelligence was manifested in the culture itself and could be assessed by making systematic observations of complex behavior. But how to systematize and what to observe? Again, he reasoned that the behavior to be observed should be that behavior from school and life that requires high-order mental processes.

---

[22]Chauncey and Dobbin, *Testing*, p. 3.

Most of it would be verbal. Binet essentially argued that since the culture itself carries the materials of intelligence, the developing child is exposed to approximately common intellectual stimuli. To the degree that individuals differentially acquire and incorporate into their behavior these materials for thinking, intelligence would be reflected. Today, one could call such an approach in testing a work sample. In this case, the work being sampled is mental. The argument is also somewhat circular in that it holds that intelligence is evident in "intelligent" behavior. It is startling how closely this reasoning can parallel the construction of classroom tests of achievement. In each instance, one starts with the need and desire to measure an abstract, complex construct. For Binet, this was intelligence. For the teacher, it is usually some aspect of achievement specified by an instructional objective. In each case, the tester sets out to capture some manifestation of the construct in which he is interested by providing cues designed to elicit behavior related to the construct. Further, standards for the performance are established so that the behavior can be judged and comparisons between individuals made.

Finally, Binet devised a means of constructing his tests which gave them inherent meaning. The way he did this was to conceive of mental ability as a growth function. Those who are more able, it was noted, can do certain things earlier than the typical child. Those who are less able do these same things later than the typical child. This reasoning is the foundation of *age scales.* In this system of scaling (and Binet followed this procedure), the researcher's problem is to find tasks which reliably differentiate age groups. If, for example, the ability to spell "cat" correctly can be demonstrated by the typical seven-year-old but not by the typical six-year-old, performance of that task could be used to differentiate the two groups of children. Now, that is fine as far as it goes, but unless spelling "cat" is relevant to the measurement of, let us say, intelligence, we run the risk of differentiating groups by the use of spurious tasks.

There are, for example, many growth functions related to age. Some of them are sensory, perceptual, emotional, physical, or intellectual. Unless one is careful in the selection of the tasks, part of any measure which is age-scaled may represent irrelevant growth. Binet dealt with all of these problems in terms of his reasoning and his procedures. What he did, in summary, was to (1) hypothesize that intelligence is developmental, (2) assume that the culture provides stimuli for intellectual growth approximately equally for all individuals, (3) assume that intelligence could be inferred from the behavior elicited by standard problems, and (4) empirically establish a system of tasks that demonstrably differentiates typical children from varying age groups.

From his initial work, many of our concepts regarding intelligence were derived. Many of our measurement methods stem from the same source. The procedures and techniques have been refined over the years, but the importance of Binet's early work can never be denied. Intelligence testing is one of the brightest chapters in applied psychology, in spite of certain misuses and limitations. Again, the practicing teacher will need to be informed about intelligence testing and its limitations. No single psychological measure can be compared to intelligence in terms of its impact upon school usage.

Other psychological constructs have not been as successfully measured. Personality, interests, temperament, creativity, and so forth have been measured, but with far less success. Given time and development, it may be that some of these measures will prove to be as useful as intelligence in the conduct of education. At this time, it is safe to say, however, that such measures are primarily in their developmental stages, with severe limitations regarding their pragmatic use.

Statistics

This section, perhaps, could more accurately be identified as "Behavior and Its Measurement," as historical development in statistics per se is of interest to us only as a tool for other purposes. These purposes and the utilization of statistical concepts for them have developed side-by-side in education and psychology while theories of behavior, the philosophy of science, and measurement theory have evolved. Numbers as used in educational measurement are signs for other things. They do not have independent meaning but must rest upon our knowledge of the "other things" and our understanding of the numbers' representational quality. To know something about this history is to gain something of an appreciation for the interdependence suggested.

Mathematics, of course, has an old and honored history in man's development. To the mathematician, the evolution of his discipline is independent of natural events. The concepts and procedures of mathematics are matters of logic and internal consistency. Their relationships to events in the real world are not of primary importance to the theoretician. However, the idea of the ancient Greeks that the world obeyed a mathematical model has had wide appeal. But as Guilford[23] says, "mathematics is an invention of man, not a discovery." It is important to grasp this distinction. It is not the responsibility of numbers to be representative. Natural scientists have, of necessity, concluded that natural phenomena can frequently be described mathematically. In this view, it is

---

[23]J. P. Guilford, *Psychometric Methods* (New York: McGraw-Hill Book Co., 1954), p. 6.

held that numbers may (or may not) represent things in the real world. In fact, this procedure—symbolic representation especially with numbers—has been a powerful tool used for understanding natural phenomena. The use of measures, particularly those associated with distance-mass-time, has yielded great gains.

But here it is worth noting that, because natural phenomena at the simplest level are directly observable, the accuracy of their symbolic representation is fairly readily verifiable. All scientific inquiry rests upon the notion of independent verification. Without such verification, it is obvious that we run the risk of describing and dealing with "private worlds." The degree to which psychologists and educators run that risk in terms of the phenomena in which they are professionally interested is a measure of the subjectivity of their science.

An interesting historical event concerning the verification of observations in the natural sciences took place in 1796. The event has had a profound effect upon both psychology and measurement. In that year, an assistant to the director of the Royal Observatory in Greenwich, England, lost his job because of his "carelessness" in recording sightings of a particular star. He made the mistake of deviating from "truth," in this case, the director's sighting, by about one second of arc. About twenty years later, a German astronomer learning of the incident, wondered about what he called the "personal equation," that is, do observers vary in their observations, and if so, by how much? The answers, upon investigation, were found to be "yes" and by considerable (for astronomy) amounts. Worse, it was found that the same observer was frequently inconsistent with himself. This incident and its subsequent investigation has been pointed to by psychologists as the beginning of interest in what is now known as individual differences.

At this point, we should recognize and appreciate the importance of individual differences. If objects, man included, did not display individual differences or unique qualities, there would be little point to measurement or evaluation. That is, if we were all alike in any characteristic, it would be pointless to evaluate or measure that characteristic. It is in differences that both evaluators and teachers find their work.

Statistical methods have developed from two distinct frames of reference. One is what we may call descriptive. The other is inferential. Descriptive procedures have been developed for the purpose of describing phenomena of interest. Usually, the phenomena are described from collections of data. An example is the arithmetic average used in reporting average heights or weights of children of a given age. The method of inferential statistics, on the other hand, deals with the making of inferences from controlled observations. It is frequently probabilistic, as, for example, in the statement that, based upon certain given weather conditions (observations), the chances are it will rain tonight. Predictions about educational achievement are similarly based upon known characteristics of individuals. Such predictions are essentially bets, and they represent inferences predicated upon cause and effect relationships. With this understanding, it is not surprising that the history of statistical methods began with an interest in probabilities, especially probabilities associated with gambling.

In the latter part of the seventeenth century, Bernoulli published a book devoted to the mathematics of chance.[24] A special model for certain kinds of chance events was developed in about 1733 by De Moivre.[25] We know this model today as the normal curve. Following this development, Gauss, who lived between 1777 and 1855, applied the curve to scientific data as a probability model. Interesting testimony to this application is given by the fact that the normal curve is frequently referred to as the Gaussian curve.

Another astronomer, a Belgian named Quetelet, gave strong support to applied statistics. He argued for the importance of keeping records for all manner of biological and social data. It is also reported that he found that, for unselected (non-biased) populations, certain anthropometric measures were often distributed according to "normal law," or the Gaussian curve.[26] In fact, Quetelet was so impressed by this tendency that he suggested that nature aimed at an ideal average man, *l'homme moyen,* but missed the mark, and deviations each side of average were the result. It is a temptation to agree that such does seem to be the case; at least, Quetelet's idea continues to have popular appeal.

Another European, Sir Francis Galton (1822-1911), familiar with Quetelet's ideas in applied statistics, became an important bridge between the earlier mathematical developments and psychology. Galton also happened to be the cousin of Charles Darwin who, at the time, held revolutionary ideas regarding heredity. Galton's desire was to solve certain problems in human heredity with the general purpose of upgrading man. Working with the ideas of Quetelet and Darwin, he set out to study man by establishing an anthropometric laboratory in 1882. He began by measuring human responses to a number of sensory and motor tests and, in some reversal of today's conventions, charged his subjects a fee as they provided data! Beyond the pioneering character of his measurement of human behavior, Galton developed new statistical techniques. The normal curve proved inadequate for his purposes, and so he invented new analytic tools. One line of attack was with crude correlational methods which, in terms of personalities, has further

[24]Ibid., p. 2.
[25]Ibid.
[26]E. G. Boring, A *History of Experimental Psychology.* (New York: Appleton-Century-Crofts, 1929).

historical interest. Galton's student and subsequent successor at the laboratory, Karl Pearson, carried on the advance of statistics, notably in correlational techniques. Another student, Charles Spearman, contributed important advances in the theory of intelligence. Further important advances to statistical theory and technique were made by another Britisher named R. A. Fisher.

The disciplines of psychology and measurement in America were linked to those in Europe by James Cattell, an American who studied with Wundt in Germany and who was influenced by the British empiricists. He founded psychological laboratories at the University of Pennsylvania and Columbia University in 1888 and 1891, respectively. E. L. Thorndike became a student of Cattell's, and both contributed to measurement and psychology in ways that importantly influence these fields today.

There were others, of course. Many events in addition to those cited in this chapter could have been mentioned here. Perhaps, on the basis of this brief history, however, the student will appreciate some of the richness of the past and its vitality for today. Obviously, evaluation and measurement continue to develop, but they will be forever influenced by their beginnings.

ADDITIONAL READING

CHASE, C. J., and LUDLOW, H. G. *Readings in Educational and Psychological Measurement.* Boston: Houghton Mifflin Co., 1966.

An excellent collection of important original papers in measurement. Topics range from technical to general. The beginning student of measurement will find a broad view of measurement problems efficiently presented in these readings.

CHAUNCEY, HENRY, and DOBBIN, J. E. *Testing: Its Place in Education Today.* New York: Harper & Row, Publishers, 1963.

Written for teachers, administrators, and school patrons. A meaningful and clear discussion of the issues in school testing today. An authoritative guide to test use.

FINDLEY, WARREN G., ed. *The Impact and Improvement of School Testing Programs,* Part II, Sixty-second Yearbook of the National Society for the Study of Education. Chicago: Distributed by The University of Chicago Press, 1963.

A comprehensive source of information on testing problems and issues. Each chapter is written by an expert who presents a series of recommendations supported by research and practice.

HOFFMANN, BANESH. *The Tyranny of Testing.* New York: Crowell, Collier & Macmillan, 1962.

A critical review of items found in standardized tests and certain test practices. It illustrates some of the pitfalls of testing and presents the position of the critics forcefully.

2

Foundations
of Evaluation

Have you ever considered the questions: What do you know? How did you get to know whatever you do know? Does knowledge change? The responsibility of fostering learning makes it mandatory that teachers consider these questions. We must somehow be able to hold honestly that not only do we teach, but that we know what to teach and why it is taught. In dealing with these questions, the teacher must make choices and must have some basis for making these choices. Instructional evaluation can provide the teacher with a sound basis on which to make decisions about these alternatives. However, the nature of instructional evaluation, reflecting as it does the nature of instruction, will be directly influenced by the teacher's conception of knowledge.

Why do we seek knowledge for ourselves, and, as teachers, desire to transmit it and the skills of acquiring it to our pupils? Why do we seek to influence any kind of change in others? We claim that planned changes in behavior are "good"; that these changes are advantageous; and, thus, that our function as facilitators of such changes is justified. But why? Two general possibilities seem clear. We *assume* that what we teach has for the learner either utility value or aesthetic value. On the one hand, we justify in terms of potential "pay-off" to the learner, and on the other, in terms of pleasure and beauty in a general sense. The first view is somewhat pragmatic and potentially scientific, the second somewhat mystical and existential. At the practical level of planning and conducting instruction, we may adopt both points of view. The process of evaluation, however, is probably more compatible with, or is, at least, more easily illustrated within, a system founded upon utility.

The Empirical View

Methods of knowing have been developed over a long period of time, and yet they are still incomplete, and knowledge about them is fallible. We as individuals utilize several methods to gain knowledge; nonetheless, certain methods, even though imperfect, seem to hold greater potential than others for us as teachers. It will be well to consider some of these methods.

One writer has suggested that man, in trying to explain his problems and in seeking understanding, has utilized five sources of knowledge: (1) authority, (2) personal experience, (3) deductive reasoning, (4) inductive reasoning, and (5) the scientific method.[1] Authority is a widespread source of knowledge, and for good reason. It short-cuts the other methods. We sometimes ask facetiously if it is necessary to reinvent the wheel. Usually, the answer is no. We are willing to exploit previous knowledge and experience, especially if it is well-established and has demonstrable utility. Without these conditions, we tend to be more skeptical, for we know that, at one time or another, authority has held that earth is the center of the universe; suffering is noble; bloodletting therapeutic; and royal judgment perfect. In education in general, and specifically in evaluation, the hand of authority is quite evident. The influences of the organization, of administrators, of curricular materials, of agencies and associations, of fellow teachers, and so forth are all, by and large, those of authority. While much of this authority is based upon experience and has utility, some does not.

Appeal to personal experience in seeking knowledge seems inescapable. In fact, it could be argued that all experience is personal and that the so-called scientific method is simply an instance of carefully structured personal experience. The difference in critical attitude and control, however, is an essential difference. We can be critical about the generalizations we derive from personal experience, but we usually are not. The current sentiment of distrust of anyone over thirty years of age is probably wise. The corollary to trust those under thirty is probably foolish. The trouble with personal experience is that it is subject to bias, to the whims of chance, and to severely limited scope. It can be a rich source of information, but it should always be controlled by an inquiring and critical attitude toward its generalizations. Otherwise, how is it that knowledge based upon *your* personal experience is always superior to *mine?*

Knowledge based upon reasoning, either deductive or inductive, has certain advantages and certain disadvantages when compared with

---

[1]D. B. Van Dalen, *Understanding Educational Research, An Introduction* (New York: McGraw-Hill Book Co., 1962).

knowledge based upon authority or personal experience. Deduction leads us to conclusions. It proceeds from general laws to specific predictions and depends upon the validity of its premises and their interelationships. Induction leads us to generalizations from particular instances, usually concrete and observable facts. It is a reasoning process which can be useful in establishing the validity of premises for deduction.

Thus, the two processes may complement each other. Bacon's use of induction provided a significant bridge from the powerful formal systems of deductive logic to the methods of science and experimentation. Essentially, he rejected the growing dependency upon premises founded upon authority and absolute truth and insisted upon establishing them from direct observation. This was, however, a costly demand because it was predicated upon perfect induction or complete enumeration. That is, the generalizations to be established required exhaustive observation of the instances upon which they were based. Since then, man has learned to use imperfect induction, and science has developed sophisticated procedures for sampling. We thus have learned to live with probabilistic statements of generalizations derived from partial observation.

The scientific method has been variously defined and discussed, but as has been suggested, it represents a marriage of the processes of induction and deduction. As we know the scientific method, and as it continues to develop, it synthesizes reason and observation. Reason, deduction, or theory in the more formal sense point the observations and fact-gathering to an empirical test of some deduction. The deduction under test is known as an hypothesis. The result is that the observations become directed toward establishing the reasonableness of an hypothesis as opposed to its absolute truth. We are, in this sense, making bets in which likelihood and probability replace absolute solutions. Importantly, our bets will be resolved on the basis of objective evidence insofar as possible. In this system, subjective personal judgment as evidence will be replaced by objective, external, verifiable facts. This is the empirical view.

Consequently, the empiricist expects to support his generalizations with facts of an observable nature. He is suspicious of personal opinion based upon vague references. He is oriented to verifiable evidence, not only in the persuasive efforts of others, but also in his own thinking. He seeks support and agreement among other dependable observers. The empiricist's position is, perhaps, easiest for us to understand when we consider the physical world. There, the distinctions between "point-at-able" evidence and opinion are clearer than when we deal with human behavior in a social context, such as in educational settings. In either case, however, the empiricists' position would be the same—that of replacing subjective private judgment with objective public evidence as far as possible. This position obviously argues for certain kinds of data in educational contexts and against other kinds of data.

Educational Measurement

For the purposes of this book, the above discussion needs to be filled in, with respect to its application in education. Of the previously discussed sources of knowledge, empiricism is the primary basis of educational measurement. This is an ideal, as the following example will illustrate. Not long ago, the writer was asked for a verbal evaluation of a student. The student was being considered for a position on the faculty of a certain university. The inquirer had some influence regarding the appointment. In short, he had a decision to make, either to support or to deny support to the student's application for the position. The encounter appeared to be social, but the intent was professional. The request for information came in the form: "What kind of student is X?" and "Will he be a good educational psychologist?" The reply was that X is a very fine young man who works hard and has good potential. The reply probably strikes the reader as being rather subjective and somewhat vague, which it was. What are the meanings of "fine," "works hard," and "has good potential"? The employment decision would, at this point, rest wholly upon faith in the evaluator's judgment.

Not long after this incident, the inevitable recommendation forms for X arrived from the university in question. The forms asked for ratings of X on a scale ranging in value from 1 to 5 (weak to outstanding) in the dimensions of scholarship, intellect, teaching effectiveness, research ability, and personal adjustment. An open-end section soliciting other comments was provided. Now we may feel that we are getting somewhere; we now know what is to be rated and upon what basis. Or do we? The meaning to be given words like "scholarship" and "intellect" is still largely a matter of subjective judgment for the evaluator, and there is no guarantee that the recipients of the ratings hold the same meanings. This could also be said of numbers standing for "weak," "outstanding," and so forth. Will the open-end comments "fix up" the ambiguities? Possibly, to some degree, but can that be counted upon? One could argue that the recommendation will be backed up by a transcript of course work which provides evidence for at least part of the evaluation. This is correct; but it must be added that the transcript contains course titles and symbols such as "Thesis—15 hours—A," "Advanced Statistics—3 hours—B," "Human Learning—5 hours—B," and so forth. What kind of data are these? What meaning is there in the titles and symbols? There are available descriptions of the courses represented by the titles and the symbols, and these may help. In addition, there are certain conventions (which we may be willing to assume are followed) that provide meaning. Nevertheless, the fact remains that there is unresolved ambiguity in the illustration.

To pursue the example further, the earlier recommendation forms were not sent to one evaluator alone; in this case, three sets of recommendations were required. While it is true that agreement (or disagreement) among evaluators provides more evidence than that resting upon one person's judgment, the fact remains that we would like less ambiguous, more meaningful and objective evidence of student X's ability. The same comments would apply for grades across courses in the transcript referred to.

To be more specific, how can we, granting the desirability to do so, obtain objective data relevant to educational behavior? The empirical view is that our data should be as objective as possible. It should consist of verifiable observations of the behavior in question. However, it does not deny the necessity for making judgments, but rather, it insists that the judgments be objectively supportable.

In most educational situations, there are, generally speaking, two lines of attack upon the problem of providing data: we can use procedures already developed, or we can create our own procedures. Tests are nothing other than attempts to provide objective, verifiable data pertaining to educational behavior. Illustrations of these two lines of attack are standardized tests and teacher-constructed tests. Many of the decisions which must be made from an educational point of view regarding the purpose and use of data are common to both kinds of procedures. Some of the techniques used in applying the two procedures may vary, but as one develops skills of evaluation, he will find that the two procedures have more in common and less that is different between them.

The act of evaluation and the process of measurement are of fundamental importance to any educational situation. Measurement, in its broad sense, should provide us the data upon which required or desirable evaluative judgments can be based. The requirements for effective evaluation will be many, but typically, they will involve making judgments about: (1) individual and class readiness for given learning experiences; (2) the effectiveness of the various educational procedures chosen for achieving instructional objectives; (3) the degree to which individuals and groups achieve instructional objectives; (4) the individualizing of educational experiences for either remedial or enrichment purposes; and (5) the validity of the instructional objectives themselves. The data to be considered for these functions may range from previously earned grades, to intelligence scores, to standardized achievement test scores, to special aptitude test scores, to performance upon teacher-constructed tests, to observational records, to products made, to interview information, to ratings of performance, and the like. Each evaluative problem, of course, presents unique and challenging questions. The principles of measurement and evaluation can be brought to bear upon these problems, but the solutions will be as varied as the contexts from which they arise.

Numbers and Scales

A commonly accepted definition of measurement is one attributed to Campbell which states that "measurement is the assignment of numerals to objects or events according to rules."[2] This definition has been the subject of much discussion by scientists, and especially by psychometricians. These discussions have led to further elaboration, and in some cases, disagreements regarding the nature of measurement. For our purposes, however, it is a useful definition that allows consideration of the nature of numbers and scales. These considerations should lead to a fuller appreciation of the process of measurement.

Objects and Events

On the face of it, Campbell's definition has three elements: (1) numerals, (2) objects and events, (3) assignment rules. Let us consider "objects and events" first. In this context, objects and events stand for the things in which we are interested. More precisely, they are characteristics of things that interest us. In education, our primary interest is in our students or pupils, but not in a general way; rather, our interest is in specific characteristics associated with them. The word "trait" is frequently used to make the distinction between the object itself and some specific aspect of that object. Although we are interested in the child himself, as educators, we will deal with him in terms of specific traits such as his reading ability or his mathematics achievement. Even more specifically, our interest is in his reading comprehension or in his understanding of mathematical concepts. There is in all this an implicit assumption. The assumption is that whatever trait interests us and for whatever objects, the objects will vary in the degree to which they possess the trait. Further, characterizing the object with respect to the trait will lead to descriptions and understandings which are useful. Conceivably, we might be interested in any number of traits of children, such as their height, weight, sex, color, intellect, motivation, various kinds of abilities, and so on. In the final analysis, our interest will be restricted to those traits which we can utilize for some legitimate educational purpose.

---

[2] S. S. Stevens, "On the Theory of Scales of Measurement," *Science*, 1946, 103, pp. 677-680.

Numerals

The word "numeral" has a less restrictive meaning than the word number. For that reason, it is more useful in Campbell's definition of measurement. In general, we may think of a numeral in measurement as a symbol "standing for" the suggested characterization of an object or event. Thus, 120 pounds stands for the weight of some particular individual, as 5′ 4″ stands for his height. "Bright" may characterize his general intelligence, or alternately, 115 I.Q. may be an index of the same trait obtained by certain describable operations. In any case, it is important to note that the symbols are abstractions. They are not the objects themselves but represent characteristics of the objects. Further, as symbols, they will have meaning only insofar as we give them meaning. Some traits and their symbols are so conventionally known that their meaning is clear through usage. Other traits and their symbols are not so well known or understood. Contrast, for example, the statement that a given twelve year old boy weighs 100 pounds with the statement that his mathematics grade last semester was C, or that his score on a recent English test was 65. Eventually, the meaningfulness of each of these symbols is made rational by specifying the "rules of assignment."

Rules

In educational measurement, assignment rules are the ground rules by which we associate the numerals or symbols to the characteristics of the objects of interest. Again, teachers are fundamentally interested in characteristics of their pupils. Because pupils and educational objectives are many-splendored things, we would expect to find a variety of measures utilized in educational settings. In every instance, however, our concern is with the accuracy of the symbols used for characterizing the traits of interest. What is desired is a degree of parallelism between the traits themselves (nature) and the structure of the symbol system (numerals). Scientists refer to this relationship as an equivalence of form or isomorphism.[3] The rules for assignment, of course, make a great deal of difference in the degree to which isomorphism is achieved. As Guilford points out, however, this degree of equivalence of form in applied measurement can be a matter of empirical test. Figure 2 represents these measurement concepts and provides two illustrative examples from physical and educational measurement.

As Figure 2 may suggest, if the traits selected and the rules of assignment "make sense," then the symbols may be used to characterize the objects and their relationships one to another. This could be tre-

---

[3]J. P. Guilford, *Psychometric Methods*. (New York: McGraw-Hill Book Co., 1954), pp. 6-7.

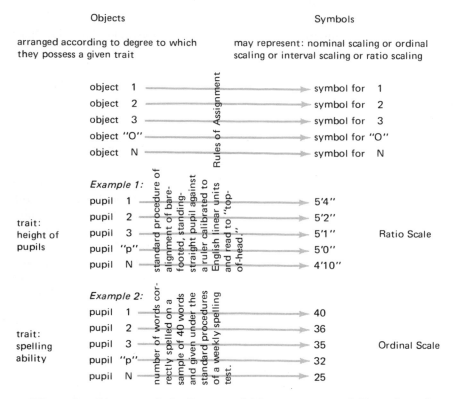

Figure 2. Diagram of the Process of Measurement, and Examples of Two Types of Scales.

mendously convenient as it would allow the abstract use of the symbol in place of the actual object for many purposes. Further, if accurate, the use of the symbols for certain traits may allow us to see the objects in ways that would otherwise be unlikely or impossible. For example, "metabolic man" was unknown until theories of metabolism and methods for measuring metabolic phenomena were developed. The same could be said of "intelligent man," "sick man," and so forth.

The availability of symbols standing for traits or characteristics is a powerful tool, but it can also be a dangerous one. We may assume unwarranted representativeness of the symbol for the object. It is tempting, especially where symbols represent human traits, to overgeneralize or to manipulate the symbols in ways that lead to misrepresentation of the traits. The subject of scaling addresses itself to this danger.

Four Types of Scales

Generally, psychometricians have identified four levels or categories of measurement. These categories are defined in terms of empirical operations associated with the traits themselves. It will be helpful to name and define each level of scaling and then illustrate. The scales are known as nominal, ordinal, interval, and ratio. The word "nominal" is derived from the Latin *nomen,* meaning "name," which suggests the chief characteristics of this scale. In nominal scaling, the basic empirical operation is a determination of equality. The numeral or symbol simply serves as a label or name for the objects classified in a given category, and all members of the category are considered equal with regard to the classification trait. To illustrate, it is common to categorize groups according to sex. The labels "male" and "female" exhaust the possibilities, and it is a simple matter to observe human beings and classify them into either of these two categories. One could as well substitute the number 1 for male and the number 2 for female as long as it is understood that 1 and 2 simply identify classes of objects considered equal with regard to sex, that is, 1 = male, 2 = female. Other nominal symbols are common, such as identification numbers, telephone numbers, ethnic classification, street names, interest groups, religious and political affiliations, and so on.

In ordinal scaling, something is added to the rules of assignment of the nominal scale. Not only must objects be distinguishable class to class, but they must be distinguishable in terms of the degree to which they possess a given trait. It must be possible to rank order the objects according to the degree to which they have the trait. For example, the old army squads frequently "fell in" or lined up according to height from an observer's left to right. In this case, it was possible to consider the soldier's left to right position given as 1, 2, 3, . . . as a symbol related to his height. Other examples are the order of finishing a race in track, academic rank at graduation, rank in a spelling bee, and so forth. In each case, one may conceptualize a trait, for example, speed, brains, and spelling ability, in which ordering is being established according to the degree to which the participants have that trait. It is important to note that differences between ordinal positions at this level of scaling do not denote known amounts of the trait in question. That is, we may be able to determine the best speller, the next best, and so on, but we do not have precise information regarding how much the spellers differ in actual spelling ability. If, as is true with many traits, most people are average, with decreasing numbers of people being extreme, we can appreciate the fact that differences in *ranks* for average people denote small differences in *amounts* as compared to people at the extremes.

Scales upon which equal differences on the scale represent equal differences in the amount of the trait are called interval scales. Operationally, this requires a demonstration of equality of intervals or differences. Elevations of points upon the earth's surface are an example. One foot of elevation is equal in meaning to any other foot in elevation, independent of the points at which the elevations are taken. Calendar time, and either Fahrenheit or centigrade temperature are further examples. The essential feature of this level of scaling is equivalence of units at any point in the scale in terms of the amount of the trait represented. One severe limitation remains, and that is the meaningfulness of zero.

In ratio scaling, zero is not simply some arbitrarily assigned point on an interval scale, but rather, it has the meaning that zero represents an absence of the trait in question. This is extremely difficult to demonstrate except in a few instances in physical measurement. In length, mass, and time (not calendar time as a representation of all historical time), we may understand zero as an absence of the trait. In little, if any, educational measurement would zero be meaningful. To illustrate, a zero I.Q. or achievement test score hardly represents the complete absence of intelligence or achievement, in spite of our temptation to so interpret them. Given, however, a meaningful zero and equal units across the scale, then strict isomorphism is achieved. That is, our symbol system would correspond to the exact amount of the traits of interest. When they are viewed in this way, we may consider the various levels of scales—nominal, ordinal, interval, ratio—as increasing degrees of isomorphism or correspondence between symbol and object.

Perhaps this discussion leads in two directions, one toward an appreciation of the fundamental nature of measurement, the other toward an awareness of some limitations and pitfalls in measurement applications. If one understands the basis for measurement, he will recognize that there are very few cases of perfect correspondence between events and traits on the one hand, and the symbols used to represent them on the other. This is true not only in the social sciences, but also in the physical sciences. Teachers and educators can, perhaps, on this basis relax to some degree their desire for absolute measures. Where ratio and interval scales are unattainable at the moment, it is quite reasonable to settle for useful nominal and ordinal measures. In view of the complex and ever-shifting focuses of interest in education, it is important to recognize that the measurement precedents from science do not suggest that meaningful zeros and equal intervals are mandatory to establish the usefulness of any and all measures. The users of check lists, ratings, product judgments, and self-devised tests can be confident in the usefulness of nominal and ordinal data. The alternative in most educational situations would be no data, a hardly acceptable alternative.

Most of us have had long experience with arithmetic and mathematics suggesting that all numbers are rational. The rational number system includes positive, negative, and fractional numbers and allows any of the four fundamental number operations. The system is an invention that extends to the operations of subtraction and division. It allows the subtraction of equal numbers by the provision of zero and the subtraction of greater numbers from lesser numbers by the provision of negative numbers. It further allows the division of numbers which are not in simple ratio by the provision of fractional values.

A number system of earlier development, the natural number system, includes only positive integers. Its operations were applicable without restriction to addition and multiplication; results are always positive integers.

Our problem is this: we are used to manipulating numbers without considering the representational meaningfulness of such manipulation to the objects described by the numbers. As one writer has said, the numbers don't complain. Given, for example, two students' I.Q.'s as 70 and 140, one may place the numbers in ratio, but it is another problem

Level of Scaling	Formal Characteristics	Visual Representation	Function	Example
nominal	mutually exclusive and identifiable categories	1 2 3	allows classification and description	race: where 1,2,3, represent white, black, brown
ordinal	rank order, more than and less than	1 2 3 4 5 6	allows the above plus ranking	test scores, where 6 is greater than 5, etc., but units represent differing amounts
interval	units have equivalent meaning throughout the scale	1 2 3 4 5 6 7 8	allows the above plus the determination and comparison of differences	elevations from arbitrarily select points, where units are equivalent throughout the scale
ratio	meaningful zero	0 1 2 3 4	allows the above plus the determination and comparison of ratios	human heights, where 3' is 1/2 of 6'

Figure 3. Comparison of Measurement Scales.

to declare that the intelligence of the one is twice that of the other; or that an upward shift of 10 I.Q. points would be equally meaningful for both. This, then, suggests that allowable manipulations of symbols in measurement are a function of the level of scaling attainable. The restrictions can be stated in terms of formal mathematical postulates, but for our purposes, less formal statements will suffice. Figure 3 contains a summarization of the concepts of scaling.

ADDITIONAL READING

ANASTASI, ANNE. *Psychological Testing*. 3d ed. New York: Macmillan Co., 1968.
> Considered to be one of the classics in psychological testing. The book provides the basic ideas of measurement elegantly and clearly.

CRONBACH, LEE J. *Essentials of Psychological Testing*. 2d ed. New York: Harper & Row, Publishers, 1960.
> A comprehensive treatment of the various types of tests found in school testing programs. The logic and rationale of measurement is provided in broad perspective.

HELMSTADTER, G. C. *Principles of Psychological Measurement*. New York: Appleton-Century-Crofts, 1964.
> A brief, well-written book which concentrates on underlying principles rather than on instruments themselves.

LINDVALL, C. M. *Measuring Pupil Achievement and Aptitude*. New York: Harcourt, Brace & World, 1967.
> A good compromise between theoretical measurement and the realities of the busy school world. Written to and for the classroom teacher.

3

The Treatment
of Empirical Data

Now that a definition of measurement and some of its theoretical implications have been discussed, we may proceed. The reader has, without doubt, in his professional as well as general experience, read articles or chapters in which data were reported. There are many procedures and techniques available for reporting data, but all have the purpose of communicating information in efficient and useful ways. To the degree that we understand these procedures and techniques, we will profit from such communication. Beyond that, as with general reading skills, improvement in our ability to comprehend contributes to our improved ability to transmit information and to conceptualize problems. This chapter is designed to present some of the most common and useful techniques for describing and interpreting data.

Description and Inference

The process of collecting and recording data serves two general purposes: (1) to facilitate description, and (2) to make inferences. Statistics, as a field of study, is sometimes subdivided into divisions concerned with descriptive and inferential techniques. Generally speaking, it may be said that the techniques of descriptive statistics provide for summarizing data in meaningful ways. The techniques of inferential statistics, in contrast, are designed for making inferences on the basis of characteristics of data. Inferential techniques, as such, usually are based upon descriptive statistics, but become more complex and theoretical. A commonly known illustration of this process is the drawing of conclusions from samples. For instance, quality control in manufacturing is usually based upon samples of products tested under controlled conditions, with the test results being used to generalize to all cases of the product in question. Customs' inspections, weather predictions, political opinions, and judgments of student achievement are all based upon notions of sampling, ranging from the very naive to the very sophisticated. Thinking of these examples may lead to an appreciation of the relatedness of descriptive and inferential processes and the fact that the terms themselves are mostly dependent upon the intent of the user. For our purposes, it will be sufficient to consider a limited number of descriptive techniques and to suggest some of their many possible uses.

Frequency Distributions and Graphs

A common situation is to have available the results of some educational measurement procedure (test) which require interpretation. So that the reader can understand how to describe and interpret data, let us assume that we have available some data. To begin then, we have simply a set of pupil names and their measures on two traits. Our task is to organize the measures into forms which will be useful to us in describing and interpreting the data at hand. Of the two sets of measures to be used as illustrative examples, one set will be relatively simple, the other somewhat more complex but probably more typical for classroom teachers.

For the simpler set of measures, suppose we assume that 10 children have had their heights measured to the nearest inch. Further, let Table

TABLE 3

Heights of Ten Children, Given to the Nearest Inch

Child	Height	Ordered Frequency Distribution		
1	60			
2	65	X	$_4$ tally	f
3	50	70	$^1_2$ 1 0	1
4	70	65	1 1	2
5	55	60	$^{1\ 6\ 7\ 9}$ 1 1 1 1	4
6	60	55	$^{5\ 8}$ 1 1	2
7	60	50	^{3} 1	1
8	55			
9	60			
10	65			

3 represent these measures, with I.D. numbers designating each child and his height given beside his identification. One of the easiest and most fundamental things we can do at this point to "make sense" of our data is to organize it into what is called a *frequency distribution*. A frequency distribution is nothing more than an ordering of the measures and an enumeration of the number of each measure. The usual principle for ordering is to list from high to low or most to least. The right side of Table 3 suggests the process by which data like that to the left may be presented as a frequency distribution. If we let X represent the values of the measures in the set and f the frequency of each value in the set, the process consists of three steps: (1) by inspection of the data, determine the values contained in the distribution and specify each value under X and in an ordered fashion—high to low; (2) tally each measure from the original unordered set beside the appropriate value in the developing distribution (in the example the tallies are identified by numbers above each indicating the order in which they were tallied); (3) add the tallies for each value and enter the sum under the f column as an indication of that value's frequency. In the finished table, it is customary to omit the tally marks as a matter of neatness, e.g.,

X	f
70	1
65	2
60	4
55	2
50	1

At this point, all of the original data is displayed, but in an ordered and efficient manner. By inspection of the frequency distribution, one may immediately determine the range of values and the incidence of each value.

Let us turn to our second set of hypothetical data. This time, we have spelling test scores for 48 pupils. The test consisted of 50 words, and the score for each pupil represents the number of words correctly spelled in the test. Let us assume that the list of words is justified in some sense as being educationally significant. The scores obtained are: 32, 36, 23, 42, 41, 46, 37, 33, 37, 28, 32, 34, 32, 20, 34, 37, 40, 45, 38, 38, 30, 34, 36, 44, 39, 38, 42, 40, 37, 31, 36, 39, 50, 39, 37, 34, 41, 39, 36, 22, 36, 41, 31, 27, 36, 45, 25, 47.

Before you look at Table 4, try to arrange these scores into a frequency distribution by the method we have just discussed. Table 4 will illustrate the value of this simple procedure for organizing numerical data.

TABLE 4

Spelling Scores for a Group of 48 Pupils Organized into Three
Alternative Frequency Distributions

Distribution A			Distribution B		Distribution C	
X	tally	f	X*	f	X*	f
50	1	1	51	1	50	1
49		0	48	1	45	5
48		0	45	4	40	14
47	1	1	42	5	35	16
46	1	1	39	9	30	7
45	11	2	36	11	25	3
44	1	1	33	8	20	2
43		0	30	3		—
42	11	2	27	2		48
41	111	3	24	2		
40	11	2	21	2		
39	1111	4		—		
38	111	3		48		
37	1111	5				
36	11111	6				
35		0				
34	1111	4				
33	1	1				
32	111	3				
31	11	2				
30	1	1				
29		0				
28	1	1				
27	1	1				
26		0				
25	1	1				
24		0				
23	1	1				
22	1	1				
21		0				
20	1	1				

*Note: X in this case designates the midpoint of the various classes.

Discrete and Continuous Data

The frequency distributions (B and C) in Table 4 are illustrations of
data grouped more coarsely. Before dealing with the details of this
grouping procedure, let us consider an aspect of the nature of data that
will help us deal rationally with the process. Variables occur in either
of two natural classifications, discrete or continuous. Phenomena which
vary in whole units are said to be discrete. Census data such as cows,
cars, and people, which are reported for enumerative purposes, are examples. In education, enrollment, attendance, book counts, desks, rooms,

schools are further illustrations. With discrete variables, our interest is in the number of units or frequency of events, and all counts are considered equivalent.

Continuous variables, on the other hand, are assumed to vary by infinitesimal amounts. Traits which are continuous are considered to be measured to the nearest unit; in other words, they represent approximate measurement. For example, measures of children's heights, weights, spelling ability, intelligence, and running speed are only useful approximations of their true measures on these traits. Probably more accurate measures could always be obtained, but we are willing to settle for a useful degree of accuracy. (In fact, researchers can be criticized legitimately for utilizing measuring procedures too precise for the purpose of the measurement.) Most traits of interest to teachers are considered continuous and include the variables achievement, aptitude, intelligence, interest, adjustment, and the like. It is important to note that although the measuring procedure may be fairly gross, as, for example, in number of test items correct, the process of measurement can still be considered to be with continuous variables. The trait, not the symbols of measurement, determines the classifications of discrete and continuous measurement.

Figure 4 contains illustrations of measuring continuous variables. Boys 1 and 2 are aligned and their heights are "read" as 60″ and 61″, respectively. These are the closest units in the illustration even though we may sense that 60″ overestimates Boy 1 and 61″ underestimates Boy 2. It should be apparent that no matter how "finely" the ruler was calibrated, we would still be making estimates to some closest "unit" even though fractional values could be employed.

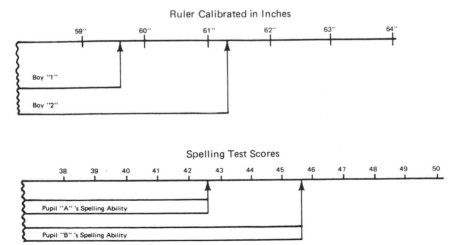

Figure 4. Illustrations of Measuring Continuous Variables.

The second part of Figure 4 suggests that traits like spelling ability can also be conceptualized as existing in "true" amounts, and that measures like the number correct on a test can be taken as approximate measures of those traits. Now it is true that the units on the spelling test probably do not have standard meaning across the scale (equidistances), but we can still maintain that A's spelling ability is estimated at 43 and B's at 46. If A and B take the same test we can also make comparisons between them in terms of their measured spelling ability.

Under some conditions, frequency distributions are organized into coarser groupings than were present in the original data. When it is recognized that the original data represents approximation and that the desired degree of precision in measurement is a function of the ability to use it, the convenience of grouping may be justified. To illustrate the procedure, the distribution from Table 4 is organized as a grouped frequency distribution in Table 5. Here it was decided to group together as a *class* scores which originally varied by one unit into sets of scores which include three adjacent units. The following diagram illustrates:

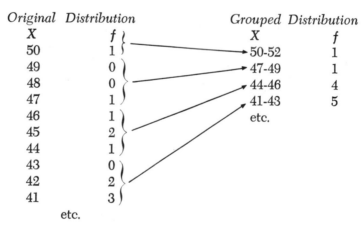

The size of the classes to be established and their limits is a matter of judgment on the part of the person reorganizing the distribution. As a general guideline, however, it must be borne in mind that the original data should not be distorted to a degree that will prove harmful in the further use of the distribution. Essentially, the judgments suggested are made to gain increased convenience within acceptable limits of distortion.

As the distributions in Table 5 suggest, there are alternate ways to display grouped frequency distributions. The values in the classes may be shown as integral limits, real limits, or midpoints. Integral limits

TABLE 5

Spelling Scores Organized as Grouped Frequency Distributions
of Three Forms

Integral Limits		Real Limits		Midpoint	
X	f	X	f	X	f
50−52	1	49.5−52.5	1	51	1
47−49	1	46.5−49.5	1	48	1
44−46	4	43.5−46.5	4	45	4
41−43	5	40.5−43.5	5	42	5
38−40	9	37.5−40.5	9	39	9
35−37	11	34.5−37.5	11	36	11
32 34	8	31.5−34.5	8	33	8
29−31	3	28.5−31.5	3	30	3
26−28	2	25.5−28.5	2	27	2
23−25	2	22.5−25.5	2	24	2
20−22	2	19.5−22.5	2	21	2

specify the lowest and the highest integers (whole numbers) contained in the class. Midpoints specify the middle value in the class and will, of course, be integers if the number of values in the class is odd, and mixed numbers if even. Real limits refer to theoretical points between which our observations are made. If, for example, we say a child's height is 60″ and we are measuring to the nearest inch, we mean that his height is closer to 60″ than to either 59″ or 61″. The theoretical limits, then, for the value 60″ are 59.5″ to 60.5″. That is, what is "seen" as 60 may in fact be any value between 59.5 and 60.5. Values beyond those limits would be "seen" as integers other than 60. Thus, the real limits of a class in a grouped frequency distribution will represent the lowest theoretical value that the lower integral limits could have and the highest theoretical value that the upper integral limit could have. The graphic scale on the following page illustrates these points from the distribution of Table 5.

Functionally, we may see that the *interval size* is determined by the distance between the upper and lower real limits within the same class; thus, 52.5 − 49.5 is 3.0. Let the symbol i represent the interval size, and we may see that i in any grouped frequency distribution is the difference between: (1) real limits within a given class, (2) midpoints from adjacent classes, (3) integral limits within the same class plus one (this is due to the fact that the integral limits are *included* in the same class), or (4) adjacent comparable points between classes. It is useful to note that upper and lower real limits are definable as the midpoint plus and minus one-half i. Symbolically we may say:

U.R.L., L.R.L. = Midpt. ± i/2.

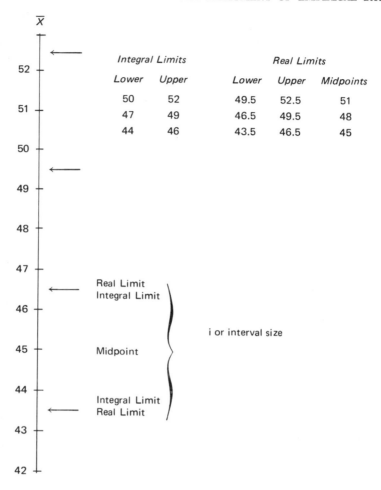

Table 6 is a reorganization of the spelling data into even coarser group-ings, with the addition of other concepts.

Sometimes in grouped frequency distributions, it is convenient to accumulate the frequencies from the bottom to the top classes into a column designated *cumulative frequency* or *cf*. This has been done in the distribution to the left in Table 6. From it, we may see that we could define the cumulative frequency for any class as:

$$\text{cf} = \text{f} + \text{cf}_{\text{below}} \tag{3.1}$$

We may view formula 3.1 simply as an instruction which tells us that the *cf* for any class is obtained by adding to the frequency of that class the cumulative frequency of the class just below it. Thus, the *cf* of the bottom class is $2 + 0 = 2$, the next $3 + 2 = 5$, etc.

TABLE 6

Grouped Frequency Distribution Incorporating Cumulative Frequencies, Relative Frequencies, and Relative Cumulative Frequencies

X	f	cf	X	rf	rcf
50	1	48	50	.021	1.000
45	5	47	45	.104	.979
40	14	42	40	.292	.875
35	16	28	35	.333	.583
30	7	12	30	.146	.250
25	3	5	25	.062	.104
20	2	2	20	.042	.042

The distribution to the right in Table 6 indicates an alternate way to treat frequencies. The column headed rf reports the frequencies in relative terms, the letters rf standing for *relative frequencies*. We may define the relative frequency for any class as:

$$rf = f/N, \text{ where N} \tag{3.2}$$

stands for the total number of scores in the distribution. This formula indicates that rf is simply an expression of the proportion of all frequencies within any given class. The rf value for the bottom class is $2/48 = .042$, for the next class $3/48 = .062$, etc. This method of reporting is useful for making comparisons among distributions on like measures but with different N's, for example, among different classrooms on the same test where the size of the groups differs. It follows that if frequencies may be reported in relative terms, so may cumulative frequencies. Thus, rcf stands for *relative cumulative frequency* and, for any class within a frequency, distribution may be defined as:

$$rcf = cf/N \tag{3.3}$$

The rcf values for the bottom two illustrative classes were obtained as $2/48 = .042$ and $5/48 = .104$.

Graphical Representation of Frequency Distributions

Graphs are very useful for representing frequency distributions; from them, we can obtain an immediate impression of the data's characteristics. Three commonly used types of graphs will help us develop additional measurement concepts of importance. They are histograms, frequency polygons, and ogives. Figure 5 contains the essential features of each of these types of graphs. The vertical axis on all three types of

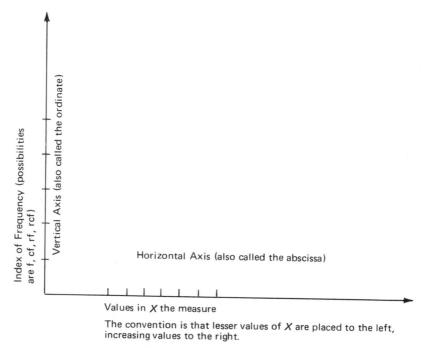

Vertical Axis (also called the ordinate)

Horizontal Axis (also called the abscissa)

Values in *X* the measure

The convention is that lesser values of *X* are placed to the left, increasing values to the right.

Figure 5.   General Model for Graphs.

graphs represents some index of frequency, and the horizontal axis is a representation of the measurement scale (X). The several possibilities and conventions are indicated in Figure 5.

Figure 6 contains three specific kinds of graphs, each being a graph of the distribution of Table 6. As may be seen, the histogram is a bar graph, with the height and sides of each rectangle determined by the frequency and real limits, respectively, of each class. Histograms offer a discrete picture of frequency distributions and are thus often used either to display discrete data or to emphasize the varying frequencies among classes.

In contrast, frequency polygons are constructed by plotting the frequencies above the midpoints for each class. Two additional classes, one just below the bottom class and one just above the top class of the distribution, are included in order to plot the zero frequencies that bring the figure to the baseline. The general picture that frequency polygons present is of more gradual change in frequencies, class to class. This serves to emphasize the continuous nature of data. We will discuss frequency polygons further after the general characteristics of ogives are considered.

Ogives are graphs of cumulative frequencies as opposed to simple frequencies. In contrast to frequency polygons, the value of the cumulative frequency for any given class is plotted over the upper real limit

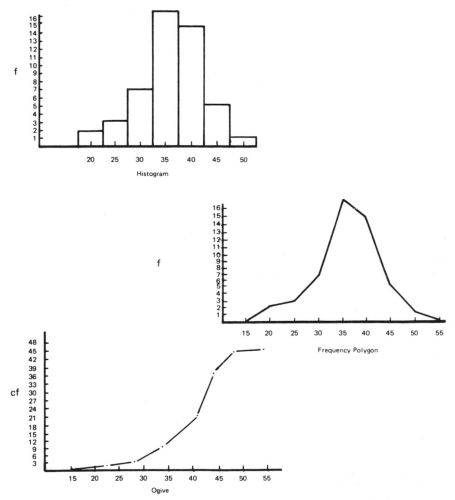

Figure 6. Illustrative Histogram, Frequency Polygon, and Ogive.

for that class. The rationale for so doing is that all frequencies in and below any particular class may be considered to have accumulated to that point regardless of how they are distributed within the class. Ogives are graphs which show the way frequencies are accumulating through the distribution. It follows from this definition that the angle of the various segments of an ogive indicates the rate of accumulation of frequencies. Therefore, ogives will present steep inclines over those classes with greater frequencies, and gentle inclines over those classes with fewer frequencies. When the ordinate for ogives is given in relative terms (rcf), the graph is a clear way to conceptualize percentiles and percentile ranks. More will be said of this in the section on ranks.

Much of the descriptive richness of statistics for describing data comes from the terminology of graphs. It is common practice that frequency polygons are free-hand smoothed to gain general impressions about distributions. When this is done, some very useful ways to describe the distributions are made possible. First, we may consider the two most general ways to characterize distributions. Any distribution may be classified as *symmetrical* or *asymmetrical*. Let us suppose that, in any smoothed frequency distribution, we can locate the center ordinate or line which divides the area under the curve into two equal parts. We shall later learn that this ordinate locates the median. Now let us imagine folding the distribution along this center ordinate. The two halves of the full distribution when so folded coincide for symmetrical distributions, and do not for asymmetrical distributions. The following diagram illustrates.

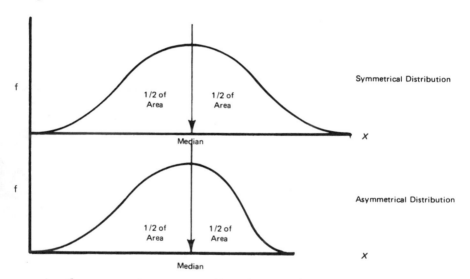

Another convenient way to describe distributions is with reference to their most common (frequent) score. The name given to the most frequent score in any distribution is the *mode*. Modes can be determined by inspecting either frequency distributions or polygons and, in smoothed distributions, are those score values identified by the tallest ordinate. *Unimodal* distributions are those with single modes; *bimodal* distributions contain two, and so on. Descriptively, the characterization of distributions may incorporate information regarding the mode and symmetry of the data. Following are four smoothed frequency polygons illustrating these points.

Often, distributions are described in terms of their overall appearance, as U-shaped, J-shaped, or rectangular. As suggested, these are gross descriptions and, in many instances, are adequate for general pur-

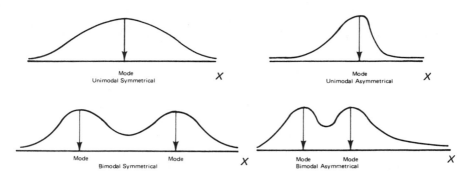

poses. Two somewhat more precise concepts are useful. They are *skewness* and *kurtosis*. Skewness pertains to the lack of symmetry, and kurtosis to the degree of peakedness of distributions. Asymmetrical distributions may be skewed either to the right or to the left. Distributions which are more peaked than the Gaussian (normal) curve are described as *leptokurtic;* those which are flatter are said to be *platykurtic.* The accompanying diagram illustrates these general classes of distributions. The normal curve will be discussed in greater detail in a subsequent section, but for the moment, we may note that it is symmetrical.

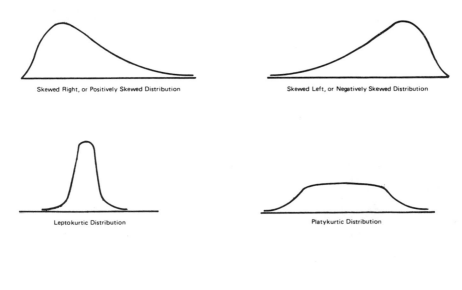

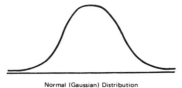

Asymmetrical distributions are described as being skewed right or left in reference to the location of their modes. That is, the direction the "stretched tail" leads determines the direction of the skew—opposite to the location of the mode. Alternatively, right and left skews are described as positive or negative because of the convention of placing higher scores to the right and lower scores to the left in graphs of distributions.

At this point, let us consider some of the interpretations that might be given to distributions in terms of the characteristics we have considered. In a general way, of course, the determination of modes indicates average performance. More precise indices of average are available, but modes are useful in roughly characterizing distributions. For example, for large representative distributions of I.Q. scores, the mode is approximately 100. One hundred is, by determination of the mode,

TABLE 7

General Types of Score Distributions, Their Characteristics
and Possible "Cause" in Educational Situations

Type	Characteristics	Possible Explanation
Positively Skewed	Mode at lower end, decreasing frequencies with increasing scores.	Test too difficult, group deficiencies, poor instruction, or trait is naturally skewed.
Negatively Skewed	Mode at upper end, decreasing frequencies with decreasing scores.	Test too easy, group exceptionally proficient, extraordinary instruction, or trait is naturally skewed.
Leptokurtic	Short range and extreme peak.	Insufficient test length or redundant items, group unusually homogeneous, influence of instruction either constant or superficial, or trait is homogeneous.
Platykurtic	Wide range or flat distribution or both.	Test very heterogeneous in difficulty of items or traits measured, group unusually heterogeneous, instruction very individualized, or trait naturally heterogeneous.
Normal	Unimodal, symmetrical, "bell-shaped," "idealized" mathematical function.	Virtually unknown in its strict form outside of theoretical discourse, approximations possible when traits, tests, and events result in a mode at the center of a distribution with successively fewer frequencies in both directions from the center of the distribution.

the most common single I.Q. value. When we consider kurtosis and its meaning, it is apparent that it is related to the variability of scores within distributions. Leptokurtic distributions are characteristic of relatively

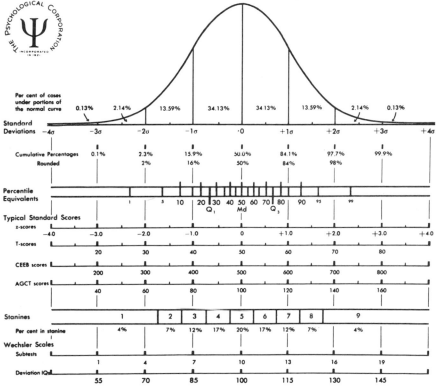

THE NORMAL CURVE, PERCENTILES AND STANDARD SCORES

Distributions of scores on many standardized educational and psychological tests approximate the form of the NORMAL CURVE shown at the top of this chart. Below it are shown some of the systems that have been developed to facilitate the interpretation of scores by converting them into numbers which indicate the examinee's relative status in a group.

The zero (0) at the center of the baseline shows the location of the mean (average) raw score on a test, and the symbol σ (sigma) marks off the scale of raw scores in STANDARD DEVIATION units.

Cumulative percentages are the basis of the PERCENTILE EQUIVALENT scale.

Several systems are based on the standard deviation unit. Among these STANDARD SCORE scales, the z-score, the T-score and the stanine are general systems which have been applied to a variety of tests. The others are special variants used in connection with tests of the *College Entrance Examination Board*, the World War II *Army General Classification Test*, and the *Wechsler Intelligence scales*.

Tables of NORMS, whether in percentile or standard score form, have meaning only with reference to a specified test applied to a specified population. The chart does not permit one to conclude, for instance, that a percentile rank of 84 on one test necessarily is equivalent to a z-score of +1.0 on another; this is true only when each test yields essentially a normal distribution of scores and when both scales are based on identical or very similar groups of people.

The scales on this chart are discussed in greater detail in *Test Service Bulletin No. 48*, which also includes the chart itself in smaller size. Copies of this *Bulletin* are available on request from The Psychological Corporation, 304 East 45th St., New York 17, N.Y.

Figure 7. Normal Curve, Its Percentile Equivalents and Related Test Scales.

homogeneous groups; platykurtic distributions are characteristic of relatively heterogeneous groups. Skewness indicates the general locations within distributions of "bunching" and "scattering." Distributions which are skewed to the right reflect a piling up at the lower end and a stretching out at the upper end of the distribution. Negatively skewed distributions would indicate the reverse characteristics. Table 7 enumerates common possible causes for some of the descriptive characteristics discussed. Teachers should bear these causes in mind when considering distributions.

Reference has been made several times to a special distribution known as the normal curve. It is a graph of a special mathematical function developed by Gauss. The distribution itself is very important in the theory of measurement. The accompanying chart is an illustration of the normal distribution and a number of derived scales which can be related to it approximately.

Normal Distributions

One way to understand the meaning of the normal distribution is to recognize that its area represents the relative incidence of events *which are normally distributed.* In this sense, the normal curve, or any other curve so used, is a model for describing a frequency distribution. To illustrate, let us suppose that the following curve is given as a model for the relative frequencies of values (dots) obtained by throwing a die, as in half a crap game. We know that, in an unbiased die, the probability of all values is equal and that, with six sides designated

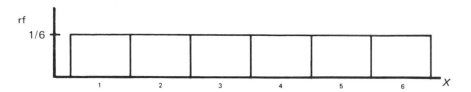

$1-6$, the probability of any value is 1/6. We can thus diagram the relative frequencies by showing a rectangular distribution, with each segment of the distribution representing 1/6 of the total area under the curve. It can also be seen that the relative frequency of sets of values can be obtained by combining the areas of the curve representing all members of the set. For example, we would expect the value 1 to be obtained 1/6 of the time. The values 1 or 2 are expected 1/3 of the time. One-half the throws should result in 1's, 2's, or 3's, etc. The figure could be altered so that fractional values are given as percents:

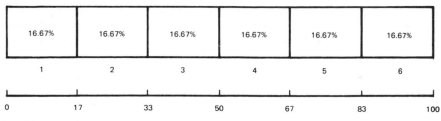

Cumulative
Percentages
Rounded

A cumulative percentage scale has been added below the figure. This scale simply indicates at selected points along the distribution the percentage expected for the indicated value plus all values below that point. Let us suppose now that the preceding figure represented some continuous trait known to be rectangularly distributed. We could use the indicated figure to describe either the relative frequency of each score $(1-6)$ or the relative rank of that score, that is, the proportion of the distribution at and below each score.

It is in this sense that Figure 7 represents the normal distribution. It is apparent that, since the normal curve is bell-shaped and symmetrical, the percentages and cumulative percentages vary for different distances, but that they are themselves symmetrical.

The importance of the normal curve to inferential statistics and the theory of measurement is fundamental. Its importance is as a mathematical model applicable to a wide range of theoretical problems. The name "normal curve" has been unfortunate in applied educational measurement for it seems to connote a widely applicable model for describing phenomena. It is true that a few traits may be approximately normally distributed. One such trait, measured I.Q., is so distributed primarily because the scales constructed to measure I.Q. were designed to yield I.Q.'s distributed normally. In the past, course grades were sometimes assigned according to frequencies dictated by the normal curve. Such practices are indefensible. It must be remembered that the normal distribution is a mathematical invention. Descriptively, it is useful as a model only when it can be demonstrated that the trait measured is itself normally distributed. Outside of theoretical discussions, such demonstrations are rare, if not unknown.

Averages

Probably the best known and most commonly used statistical concept is the average. Arithmetic averages are used to describe a wide variety of phenomena in everyday life. In measurement, there are three commonly used indices of central tendency or averages. They are the *mode*, the *mean*, and the *median*. In the section dealing with graphs, we defined the mode as the most frequent score in a distribution. In our example, the modal height of the children was 60″, and the modal spelling score was 36 words. As an index for typifying sets of data, the mode has limitations. If, for example, distributions are neither unimodal nor symmetrical, the mode can be rather meaningless. This is explained by the fact that it is mathematically unrelated to all other scores in the distribution. The mode may be largely a matter of chance in any distribution and thus is considered unstable. Both the mean and the median are more precise in this sense.

There are several kinds of means used by statisticians for different purposes, but the most common and generally useful is the arithmetic mean. We will understand that the term *mean* is the arithmetic mean and define it as the sum of a set of measures divided by the number of measures in the set. Symbolically we define the mean as:

$$\bar{X} = \frac{\Sigma X}{N}, \text{ where} \tag{3.4}$$

$\bar{X}$ is the mean,

Σ is the summation sign indicating add all X's,

X is each of the measures in the set, and

N is the number of measures added.

Using the set of height measures in Table 3 to illustrate, formula (3.4) is applied as:

$$\bar{X} = \frac{60 + 65 + 50 + 70 + 55 + 60 + 60 + 55 + 60 + 65}{10}$$

$$= \frac{600}{10} = 60$$

It may occur to the reader that a more convenient procedure for computing the mean could be attained from grouped frequency distributions. If we let the midpoint of each class represent all scores in that class, then subtotals for each class could be obtained by multiplying the frequency for each class times its midpoint. Adding these subtotals would then be analogous to adding all individual scores. To illustrate, using the same data as before:

X	f	fX
70	1	70
65	2	130
60	4	240
55	2	110
50	1	50
	N = 10	ΣfX = 600

A formula for computing means from grouped frequency distributions may be given as:

$$\overline{X} = \frac{\Sigma fX}{N} \qquad (3.5)$$

To continue the illustration, formula (3.5) would be applied to our data as:

$$\overline{X} = \frac{70 + 130 + 240 + 110 + 50}{10} = \frac{600}{10} = 60.$$

In this case, the value of the mean using either formula is the same; but if there is misrepresentation associated with the substitution of the midpoint for the original ungrouped scores in the class, then grouping error arises. Thus, there is a question raised in reference to the advantages gained from grouping procedures vs. the importance of grouping errors. Usually, we are willing to risk some grouping error for the gain in convenience, especially when we recognize the approximate character of the original scores. The earlier example of spelling test scores may provide a more realistic example of the use of grouping procedures. The sum of the original ungrouped spelling scores is 1737; thus, the mean as obtained by (3.4) is:

$$\overline{X} = \frac{\Sigma X}{N} = \frac{1737}{48} = 36.1875.$$

Earlier, the spelling scores were grouped into two different frequency distributions with i = 3 and 5, respectively.

X	f	fX	X	f	fX
51	1	51	50	1	50
48	1	48	45	5	225
45	4	180	40	14	560
42	5	210	35	16	560
39	9	351	30	7	210
36	11	396	25	3	75
33	8	264	20	2	40
30	3	90		N = 48	$\Sigma fX = 1720$
27	2	54			
24	2	48			
21	2	42			
N = 48		$\Sigma fX = 1734$			

Following these examples, the application of (3.5) for the distribution where i = 3:

$$\overline{X} = \frac{\Sigma fX}{N} = \frac{1734}{48} = 36.125$$

and where i = 5:

$$\bar{X} = \frac{\Sigma fX}{N} = \frac{1720}{48} = 35.8333. \ldots$$

In these illustrations, we may see that the grouping error, although relatively small, is likely to increase as a function of the coarseness of grouping.

Granting the relative facility by which means may be computed using grouped data, it can still be a rather tedious procedure. To reduce the arithmetic burden, a simple method is available which can aid the teacher lacking access to calculators and computers. Essentially, the procedure is based upon the device of substituting a relatively simple arbitrary scale for the original score scale, calculating in terms of the simpler scale, and finally, transposing the result back to the original scale. If, for example, we wished to determine the mean of the scores 27, 28, 29, 30, 31, we could divide the sum of the scores, 145, by 5 and obtain 29. But, we could also assign the values 0, 1, 2, 3, 4 to the original scores, divide this sum, 10, by 5 and obtain 2. We can see that 2 here represents 2 "units" above zero which in the original set was 27; thus, 27 + 2 = 29. We can conceptualize this process as equating two scales, X the original scale, and a "coded" scale d; determining the relationship between the scales; computing the mean in the simpler scale; and finally, translating the result back to X value in terms of the relationship between X and d. Diagramatically, the procedure for grouped distributions could be represented as:

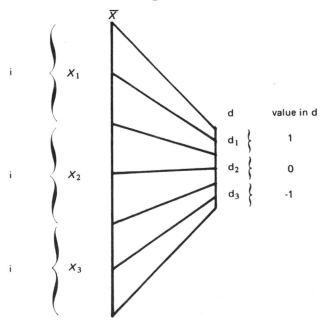

It is evident that two constants determine the relationship between X and d, namely the value of X associated with 0 in d, and the size of "units" in X (i) compared to "units" in d. If we compute the mean in terms of d, it would be equal to $\frac{\Sigma fd}{N}$ as analogous to $\frac{\Sigma fX}{N}$. If we always use unit steps in d (. . ., -2, -1, 0, 1, 2, $\cdots$) to represent successive intervals (i), then it follows that $i \frac{(\Sigma fd)}{N}$ adjusts the mean d value back to X "units." Finally, if we add back the value of X equivalent to 0 in d, we adjust for the "displacement" between the scales. This reasoning leads to a formula for determining means by coded procedures.

$$\overline{X}_d = i \frac{(\Sigma fd)}{N} + A.R., \text{ where} \tag{3.6}$$

$\overline{X}_d$ represents the mean obtained by code from d

$\frac{\Sigma fd}{N}$ is simply the mean on the d scale

i is the multiplier to adjust units between the scales

A.R. is the value of X set equal to zero in d.

Applying formula (3.6) to our spelling illustration, we would proceed as:

X	f	d	fd	X	f	d	fd
51	1	5	5	50	1	3	3
48	1	4	4	45	5	2	10
45	4	3	12	40	14	1	14
42	5	2	10	35	16	0	0
39	9	1	9	30	7	−1	−7
36	11	0	0	25	3	−2	−6
33	8	−1	−8	20	2	−3	−6
30	3	−2	−6		N=48	$\Sigma fd = 27 - 19 = 8$	
27	2	−3	−6				
24	2	−4	−8				
21	2	−5	−10				
	N=48	$\Sigma fd = 40 - 38 = 2$					

$\overline{X}_d = i \left(\frac{\Sigma fd}{N}\right) + A.R.$

$\quad = 3\left(\frac{2}{48}\right) + 36$

$\quad = 6/48 + 36 = 0.125 + 36$

$\quad = 36.125$

$\overline{X}_d = i \left(\frac{\Sigma fd}{N}\right) + A.R.$

$\quad = 5\left(\frac{8}{48}\right) + 35$

$\quad = \frac{40}{48} + 35 = 0.833\ldots + 35$

$\quad = 35.833\ldots$

It will be noted that the means so obtained are identical to those earlier obtained by formula (3.5). This will always be the case, barring computational error. The procedure is applicable for any i or A.R., a matter which can be confirmed by experimentation with various frequency distributions. The savings in computational time and effort are worth the time necessary to master the use of formula (3.6). This claim can also be confirmed by experimentation.

The mean is a generally useful index of central tendency. It is easily and commonly understood. The usual meaning for the term average is the mean, whether the context is baseball, temperature, income, intelligence, or achievement. The mean does have one characteristic that should be better understood. It is influenced by extreme scores in distributions. This can readily be appreciated by recognizing its direct relationship to the sum (total) of the values in the distribution. In skewed distributions, the mean is directly influenced by the few extreme scores and, thus, by itself, can be a misleading index for certain purposes. For example, the mean of the set of scores 3, 4, 5 is 4. Add to the set the score 16, and the mean becomes 7, an index which characterizes the set rather badly.

Median

The *median* is an index of central tendency which is less subject to the influence of extreme scores. The median is defined as the middle score in an ordered distribution. It is determined by count through the distribution. If there is an odd number of scores, the median is the midscore; if there is an even number of scores, the median is, by convention, taken to be half-way between the two midscores. Therefore, the median of the scores 3, 4, 5 is 4, the midscore; when the score 16 is added to the set, the median becomes, by convention, 4.5 which is half the distance between the two midscores of 4 and 5. The reader may wish to determine the medians of the height and spelling distributions for practice.

Ranks and Relative Ranks

We earlier discussed some of the basic problems in measurement, problems which prohibit the direct interpretation of test scores. For example, the absence of meaningful zeroes and the inequality of units across scales are important limitations. In educational practice, it is apparent that test scores are a function of the difficulty of test items as well as the ability of the examinee. These considerations have led to the development of scales which indicate the ranking of performances. The rationale for this is that if we know something about the performance called for in a test and something about the group taking the test, then scores reported as ranks within the group will have meaning.

Let us suppose, for example, that we know that a given student received a raw score of 40 on a spelling test. What does this indicate about the spelling ability of the student? Knowing that there were 50 words to spell does not help much. By looking at the words to be spelled, we might be able to make some additional judgments; but knowing what group the student belongs to would help even more. Forty words correct out of a given 50 for third graders might have a different meaning than 40 words correct out of a given 50 for graduate students. After specifying a meaningful group to which the student belongs, we must consider that the score 40 will still be a function of the difficulty of the words. A list containing cat, cow, cap, and words of comparable simplicity is quite different from a list containing cinnabar, cirrhosis, clepsydra, and the like.

One useful way to give raw scores meaning is to specify the relative rank of the score in terms of the scores obtained by other members of a relevant group. Classroom groups provide, for many purposes, legitimate comparison groups. This is not to say that special factors, such as handicaps and special abilities, should be ignored. It is to say, that as a beginning point, it is useful to determine the performance of pupils relative to other pupils receiving roughly comparable instruction. For example, if we know that a pupil earns spelling scores equivalent to the median spelling score earned by his classmates, we could interpret his performance as being average for his group. Similarly, we may be able to determine those who are above and those who are below average. Obviously, we may wish to take other factors into account in the evaluation of spelling, but the fact remains that specifying the relative performance of pupils is meaningful. Procedures for precisely determining relative ranks are useful in applied measurement and, once mastered, add significantly to an understanding of test norms.

Percentile Ranks

Let us begin by providing two definitions. The *percentile rank* (PRK) of a score in a distribution is the percent of measures below the given score. A *percentile* (P) is the score below which some given percent of the distribution falls. In the usual classroom situation, we would probably be interested in determining the percentile ranks of an obtained distribution first and later describing the distribution in terms of selected percentiles. For our purposes, we will consider simplified procedures which are valid and assume that readers interested in more general methods can find them through the bibliography. Let us assume that the typical teacher's purposes will be served if we con-

TABLE 8

Distribution of Height Measures Illustrating Percentile Ranks

X	f	cf	cf'	PRK
70	1	10	9.5	95
65	2	9	8.0	80
60	4	7	5.0	50
55	2	3	2.0	20
50	1	1	0.5	5
45	0	0		
	N = 10			

sider only the problem of determining percentile ranks for midpoints in grouped frequency distributions. That being the case, let us consider the distribution in Table 8.

The meanings of the first three columns in the table are familiar to the reader. The fourth column (cf') is a device based upon an assumption which leads directly to obtaining the percentile rank (PRK). Let us consider the definition of PRK. In order to establish PRK's, we will need to determine the number of scores which fall below each of the midpoints in the distribution and, also, somehow to resolve the question as to how many of the f's within the midpoint's class should be considered to be below the midpoint. Recalling the discussion of approximate measurement, we may reasonably assume that half the scores within any class are below the midpoint and that half are above it. Let us then define cf' as the cf below any class, plus 1/2 of the f in the class. Thus, cf' is a direct statement of the frequencies known and assumed to be below the midpoint of each class within a frequency distribution. The next step in determining PRK would then be to determine what percent each cf' is of the total distribution (N). Using these definitions:

$$\text{PRK of } X = \frac{\text{cf}'}{N} \cdot 100 \tag{3.7}$$

Table 9 is an application of these procedures to the previously used spelling scores grouped with intervals of 1 and 3. The reader may wish to verify selected PRK's in these distributions as a procedure for mastering the use of (3.7). The procedure as outlined is applicable to frequency distributions regardless of the interval selected or the trait

TABLE 9

Percentile Ranks Determined for Spelling Score Distributions

	i = 1					i = 3			
X	f	cf	cf'	PRK	X	f	cf	cf'	PRK
50	1	48	47.5	98.94	51	1	48	47.5	98.94
49	0	47	47	97.90	48	1	47	46.5	96.86
48	0	47	47	97.90	45	4	46	44	91.65
47	1	47	46.5	96.86	42	5	42	39.5	82.28
46	1	46	45.5	94.78	39	9	37	32.5	67.70
45	2	45	44	91.65	36	11	28	22.5	46.87
44	1	43	42.5	88.53	33	8	17	13	27.08
43	0	42	42	87.49	30	3	9	7.5	15.62
42	2	42	41	85.40	27	2	6	5	10.42
41	3	40	38.5	80.20	24	2	4	3	6.25
40	2	37	36	74.99	21	2	2	1	2.08
39	4	35	33	68.74					
38	3	31	29.5	61.45					
37	5	28	25.5	53.12					
36	6	23	20	41.66					
35	0	17	17	35.41					
34	4	17	15	31.25					
33	1	13	12.5	26.04					
32	3	12	10.5	21.87					
31	2	9	8	16.66					
30	1	7	6.5	13.54					
29	0	6	6	12.50					
28	1	6	5.5	11.46					
27	1	5	4.5	9.37					
26	0	4	4	8.33					
25	1	4	3.5	7.29					
24	0	3	3	6.25					
23	1	3	2.5	5.21					
22	1	2	1.5	3.12					
21	0	1	1	2.08					
20	1	1	0.5	1.04					

measured. In the usual classroom application, i will be one. Note that where f equals zero in two adjacent classes, the PRK's for those values of X will be equal. This is a matter of definition, as is the entire procedure. It may be well at this point to recall the definition of PRK and contemplate its basic meaning. PRK's are nothing more than the relative ranks of scores in a distribution. As such, they do not identify the cause or meaning of performance. To gain such meaning, we would have to consider judgmentally the nature of the performance and the group within which it occurred. These are evaluative questions.

One further comment should be made regarding the data in Table 9. It will occur to some that the reporting of PRK's to two decimal places is not justified in the example using the procedure outlined. This is a question of the number of digits which are meaningful (significant) in given situations. In order for us to learn to use relative ranks, we will ignore that problem and simply say that, for most classroom applications, rounding PRK's to two digits is conventional. Therefore, in the first distribution (i = 1), we would probably assign PRK's of 75, 69, 61, 53, etc. to the scores 40, 39, 38, 37, etc. Accepting this, we are ready to consider a simplified procedure for determining percentiles.

Percentile Ranks and Percentiles Differentiated

The reader will recall that percentiles (P) were defined as score points below which given percents of a frequency distribution fall. They are score points dividing a distribution into desired parts from the bottom up. To clarify, the median is a special percentile dividing the bottom and top halves (50%) of the distribution. Other special percentiles of interest are the quartiles [three points dividing the distribution into 4 equal parts (25%)] and the deciles [nine points, 10 equal parts (10%)]. Figure 8 illustrates the quartiles, and the accompanying ogive generalizes. That is, it is apparent that distributions may be divided into any number of equal parts desired. What is essential to recognize is that the points of division are *determined* by proportions (or percents) of the frequencies, but the points are specified in terms of score (X) value. Thus, the *scores* at P_{25}, P_{50}, P_{75} are percentiles. To make the distinction between percentiles and percentile ranks, if we were interested in determining P_{40} from the ogive of Figure 8, we start with the given relative rank (40% of distribution below) and proceed in the direction of the arrows to X_1. X_1's value is P_{40}. In contrast, if we wish to determine the percentile rank of X_2, we begin with the given score value and proceed in the opposite direction to determine the relative rank. General procedures and formulas are available for doing this, but as has been suggested, simplified methods will be sufficient for our purposes. We have dealt with percentile ranks; let us now consider percentiles.

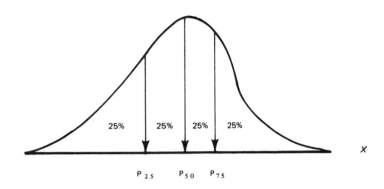

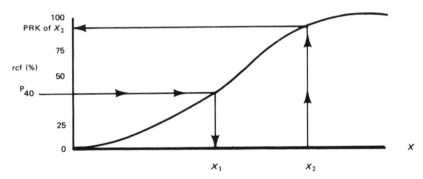

Figure 8. Illustration of Quartiles and an Ogive Differentiating PRK and P.

Percentiles

We will assume that PRK's have been determined for either each score in a frequency distribution $(i = 1)$, or each midpoint if the distribution is grouped $(i > 1)$. Further, we will assume that the teacher or other interested person wishes to determine selected percentile values, such as the quartiles, for purposes of describing the distribution. Thus, it is given that the teacher knows the percentile values to be determined. Our method of determination under these conditions will simply be one of interpolation. Table 10 illustrates the process of so determining the median (P_{50}) from the two sets of data $(i = 1$ and $i = 3)$ of Table 9. In Table 10, we consider only those classes immediately above and below the desired percentile, in this case P_{50}. These classes may be found by inspection of the PRK column. Here we have rounded the PRK's to whole percents. The interpolation process then consists of: (a) determining the distance between the bracketing score points, (b) determining the distance between the bracketing PRK's associated with these score points, (c) determining the distance from the lower of the two PRK's and the desired PRK, (d) determining the proportion of the distance between the bracketing PRK's that the desired distance is, (e) taking that same proportion of the available score distance, and (f) adding that proportion of score distance to the score point from which the interpolation proceeded. These steps are identified and illustrated in Table 10 by the letters used in this description. The differences between the values of P_{50} is explained, of course, by grouping and rounding error. To provide further illustrations and practice, we will determine the first and third quartiles (P_{25} and P_{75}) from the grouped distribution of Table 9, using rounded PRK values.

	X	PRK	Desired Distance	
P_{25}:	33	27		$P_{25} = (9/11 \cdot 3) + 30$
			25	$= 2.5 + 30 = 32.5$
	$\dfrac{30}{3}$	$\dfrac{16}{11}$	$\dfrac{16}{9}$	

	X	PRK	Desired Distance	
P_{75}:	42	82		$P_{75} = (7/14 \cdot 3) + 39$
			75	$= 1.5 + 39 = 40.5$
	$\dfrac{39}{3}$	$\dfrac{68}{14}$	$\dfrac{68}{7}$	

TABLE 10

Diagrammed, Step-by-Step Examples for
Determining Percentiles by Interpolation

	i = 1				i = 3		
	X	PRK	Desired Distance		X	PRK	Desired Distance
(a) ⎡37 (b) ⎡53			← 50⎤ (c)	(a) ⎡39 (b) ⎡68			← 50⎤ (c)
⎣36 ⎣42			42⎦	⎣36 ⎣47			47⎦
differences 1 11			8	differences 3 21			3

	(d)	(e)	(f)			(d)	(e)	(f)
P_{50}	= (8/11 · 1)	+ 36		P_{50}	= (3/21 · 3)	+ 36		
	= .7 + 36				= .4 + 36			
	= 36.7				= 36.4			

Although not very elegant, we could state the process as a formula with the meaning of the terms defined by the preceding discussion.

$$P = (\frac{\text{distance to desired PRK}}{\text{PRK distance}} \cdot \text{Score distance}) + \text{lower score}$$

value (3.8)

Applying (3.8) to obtain two more selected percentiles from the grouped distribution of Table 9, we have:

$$P_{70} = (2/14 \cdot 3) + 39 = 0.4 + 39 = 39.4$$
$$P_{40} = (13/20 \cdot 3) + 33 = 1.9 + 33 = 34.9$$

To summarize the discussion of ranks and relative ranks, it is clear that percentile ranks and percentiles are statements of relative position within a reference group. As such, they are easily interpretable. They express comparative standing in a direct way. At the same time that they are easily interpretable, they can easily mislead. In extremely homogeneous groups, minor changes in scores result in major changes in percentile ranks. Conversely, in extremely heterogeneous groups, major changes in scores may result in minor changes in rank. Further, relative ranks simply report "position." They never directly suggest why a given pupil or group ranks as it does. When interpreting normative scores (ranks), teachers will need to ask searching questions regarding the characteristics of the groups and the nature of the performance—the tasks—upon which they are established.

Variability

The most fundamental and pervasive characteristic of all natural phenomena is their variability. Human traits are certainly no exception; and yet it seems that the variability of human performances is more frequently overlooked than recognized. We simplify thing in terms of average, usually failing to recognize that "average" is an abstraction characterizing everyone and no one. In education, there is a history of lip service to what is called "individual differences." And yet when we talk of the realities of variability, such as the standard deviation, teachers seem to become uncomfortable if not defensive. This is unfortunate and probably unnecessary. The concepts of variation are not difficult when some effort toward understanding them is expended.

For purposes of discussion, let us suppose that we are to evaluate two offensive lines of opposing football teams designated A and B. Among other things, we are interested in the weights of the linemen as a crude index of their power and strength. We will assume that both teams use seven-man lines and that each line averages 200 pounds. On the surface, it would appear that teams A and B are well matched in terms of weight. But suppose that, "end to end," team A weighs 190, 210, 200, 200, 200, 210, and 190, and that team B weighs 210, 200, 190, 200, 180, 250, and 170. We can now see that they are not even at all with respect to weight. Team A has two linemen slightly above and two linemen slightly below its average. Team B, on the other hand, has one player appreciably above and one slightly above average and two substantially below and one slightly below average. It is easy to see that team B has a far more variable line than team A in terms of weight. What would this likely mean in performance? The student of football would see many implications that the rest of us would barely appreciate, but it is evident that, when we think of using unbalanced formations, pulling guards, and using other strategies and "stunts," these two teams could perform very differently. The classroom teacher is typically confronted with an even more bewildering situation regarding variation in performance, ability, interest, motivation, and all the rest. In order to teach well, the teacher must understand classroom variability.

To conceptualize better what the term *variability* means in measurement, we may think of synonyms such as dispersion, scattering, spread, and differences. The term *variability*, itself, simply means the differences found among measures in a distribution. It is a general term which can be defined more precisely in two general ways. In seeking indices of dispersion, statisticians have developed *range* and *deviation* indices.

Range Indices

The first class of indices includes the range itself which is:

$$R = \text{Hi} - \text{Lo} \tag{3.9}$$

That is, the range is the difference between the high and the low scores in a distribution. The range of weights for team A's line is $210 - 190$ or 20, and for team B, $250 - 170$ or 80. The range is a crude index of variation as it obviously takes into account only the two extreme measures in any distribution. Should either of these measures be atypical (a very likely event), the range is not very useful in characterizing the distribution's variability. For this reason, other range indices have been used. These range indices employ the difference between selected percentiles, such as: $P_{99} - P_{01}$, $P_{90} - P_{10}$, $P_{75} - P_{25}$. The last interpercentile difference ($P_{75} - P_{25}$) is frequently used and has the name *interquartile range*. As a further refinement of this index, the *semi-interquartile range* (Q) is defined as:

$$Q = \frac{P_{75} - P_{25}}{2} \tag{3.10}$$

Q is often seen in the description of norms for standardized tests. As can be seen, it is simply one-half the interquartile range. Justification for its use is that it is fairly stable since the points P_{75} and P_{25} represent the extremes of the "mid-range of talent," and that division by 2 further stabilizes it. Its use obviously requires the computation of two percentiles, but once this is done, Q is readily obtained and easily interpreted. Q values obtained for groups which may be legitimately compared upon similar measures (such as a common test) are directly comparable. As is easily seen, we assume that the group with the larger Q is the more variable in the trait measured. For example, Q for the weights of the lines of teams A and B are 6.375 and 12.5, respectively.

Deviation Indices

The second general class of variability indices is called *deviation indices*. Of the several specific indices of this type used, we shall consider two: the variance and the standard deviation. This can be justified because of the fact that far and away the most common index of variability in use is the standard deviation, and the variance is its"parent."

In order to understand these indices, we will begin with a very simple set of measures. Let us assume that we have just timed four children in the solution of an arithmetic story problem. Given the condition that each child correctly solved the problem, we are willing to assume that speed of solution is a crude index of their achievement. We will suppose that two of the children required 2 minutes and two required 8 minutes to solve the problem. We may treat these measures as a distribution and organize it as:

X	f
8	2
2	2

From this, we may readily see that the sum of the measures (ΣX) is: $8 + 8 + 2 + 2 = 20$; and that $\overline{X}$ is $20/4 = 5$ minutes. Using the mean score as a reference point for all measures, we see that two are three units above and two are three units below their mean. Statisticians call these last suggested measures *deviations* and define them as:

$$x = X - \overline{X} \qquad (3.11)$$

That is, x for an individual will be the difference between that individual's raw score (X) and the mean ($\overline{X}$) for the set of scores to which the individual belongs. This is a handy way to transform scores, since all distributions have a mean, and that point (the mean) can be more meaningful as a reference point than zero which, as we have seen, is often arbitrary and meaningless. Let Figure 9 represent the given situation. As can be seen, the mean, $\overline{X}$, is the "center" of the distribution. In fact, the mean is always the arithmetic center of any distribution just as the sum of the deviation scores (Σx) is always zero. Without formal proof, this can be shown to be the case in *any* distribution by

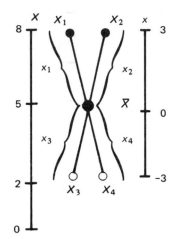

Figure 9. The Relationship between Raw Scores and Deviation Scores.

determining $x = X - \overline{X}$ values for all scores (barring rounding error) and summing them. From the figure, it is apparent that, when we define x, we simply re-refernce all X's, but that their dispersion is unaffected. That is, the *differences* between scores are equal whether the scores are given as x or X. With a little imagination, we may visualize that the x values will represent in any distribution the variability of that distribution. With more variable distributions, the distances represented by the x's will be greater. With more homogeneous distributions, those distances will be less.

There are two problems to be considered before we define the variance using these concepts. One is that, as we have said, $\Sigma x = 0$ will always be the case, no matter what the variability. The other is that the distances represented by x will not only be a function of the dispersion, but, for the entire distribution, will also be a function of the number of scores (N). The first problem has been resolved by squaring the deviations (x^2) which, as will will be recalled from algebra, always results in a positive number. The second problem has been resolved by finding the average of the squared deviations for the distribution. We may now define the *variance* (s^2) as:

$$s^2 = \frac{\Sigma x^2}{N} \text{ , where} \tag{3.12}$$
$$x = X - \overline{X}$$

To apply (3.12) to our example, we may see:

Original measures X: 8, 8, 2, 2 their $\overline{X} = 5$
Deviation measures x: 3, 3, −3, −3 from $X - \overline{X}$
Deviations squared x^2: 9, 9, 9, 9 $\Sigma x^2 = 36$

The variance $s^2 = \dfrac{\Sigma x^2}{N} = 36/4 = 9$

It is important, at this point, to appreciate the fact that the more variable a distribution is, the larger will be Σx^2, and consequently s^2. To illustrate this, let us assume that the same four children who solved the arithmetic problem before do so again. The amount of time each requires to solve the problem this time is given as:

Raw score $\qquad$ X: 5, 5, 1, 1 $\quad$ thus $\overline{X} = \dfrac{12}{4} = 3$

Deviations $\qquad$ x: 2, 2, −2, −2

Deviations squared $\quad x^2$: 4, 4, 4, 4

The variance $\qquad$ $s^2 = \dfrac{16}{4} = 4$

From these contrived examples, we can see that s^2 does indeed reflect the variability of the measures in distributions.

Another not quite so obvious problem does present itself, however, when we use the variance for descriptive purposes. When there are measurement units associated with the raw scores (as there always are whether we name them or not), such as inches, or minutes, or number of test items correct, the same units are associated with the deviation measures. Squaring the deviations results in a number of squared units, such as square inches, square minutes, square number of test items correct, and so forth. Aside from the fact that we frequently do not know how to interpret such measures, we now have an index in units other than the original measures. If this problem is difficult, its solution is simple. By taking the square root of the variance, an index of variability which is in the same units as the original measures is directly obtainable. This index is called the *standard deviation* and is defined as:

$$s = \sqrt{s^2} \qquad\qquad (3.13)$$

To determine the standard deviations of the two distributions of "time to solve an arithmetic problem," we take the square roots of the two variances of: $\sqrt{9} = 3$ and $\sqrt{4} = 2$. Again, we see that the more variable a distribution is, the larger will be its standard deviation. For our purposes, this is a sufficient means for the interpretation of s, that is, s is an index of variability which is useful for comparative descriptive purposes.

It may have occurred to the reader that the definitions provided by (3.12) and (3.13) for the variance and standard deviation are adequate for conceptual purposes, but that they would be awkward to apply for computational purposes. In any distribution where $\overline{X}$ is a mixed number (whole number with a decimal fraction), all deviations would be mixed numbers. The determination of such values, squaring and summing them, and then extracting their square root presents a laborious computational prospect. Methods for simplifying the process have been developed and will be given now. These methods can be demonstrated to be valid by mathematical proof. We shall simply give them to be accepted on faith and confirmed by example. The interested reader can find proofs in many elementary statistics textbooks.

The basis for the computational formulas to be given here is the same as that which was given for computing the mean from a coded scale (formula 3.6). That is, computations can be made in an arbitrarily assigned but simpler scale than the original scale and then "translated" back to the original scale. The following formulas are given for the variance and standard deviation determined for grouped frequency distributions with coded scales.

$$s^2 = i^2 \left[\frac{\Sigma fd^2}{N} - \left(\frac{\Sigma fd}{N} \right)^2 \right] \tag{3.14}$$

$$s = \sqrt{s^2} \tag{3.13}$$

To illustrate and confirm their comparability to the basic formulas (3.12) and 3.13), we shall apply them to the distributions of "time to solve an arithmetic problem." It will be remembered that the conventions followed for these coded formulas are to assign a unit step scale (d) to the original scale X, to compute with d values, and then translate back to X. This last step is accounted for in (3.14) by the factor i^2 which is the interval size in the grouped frequency distribution for X. Following this procedure, then, our examples are:

Time to Solve an Arithmetic Problem

Initial Measure					Second Measure				
X	f	d	fd	fd²	X	f	d	fd	fd²
8	2	1	2	2	5	2	1	2	2
2	2	0	0	0	1	2	0	0	0

$$\Sigma fd = 2 \quad \Sigma fd^2 = 2 \qquad\qquad \Sigma fd = 2 \quad \Sigma fd^2 = 2$$

$$s^2 = i^2 \left[\frac{\Sigma fd^2}{N} - \left(\frac{\Sigma fd}{N} \right)^2 \right]$$

$$s^2 = 6^2 \left[\frac{2}{4} - \left(\frac{2}{4} \right)^2 \right] \qquad\qquad s^2 = 4^2 \left[\frac{2}{4} - \left(\frac{2}{4} \right)^2 \right]$$

$$= 36 \left[\frac{1}{2} - \frac{1}{4} \right] \qquad\qquad = 16 \left[\frac{1}{2} - \frac{1}{4} \right]$$

$$= 36 \left[\frac{1}{4} \right] \qquad\qquad = 16 \left[\frac{1}{4} \right]$$

$$= \underline{\underline{9}} \qquad\qquad = \underline{\underline{4}}$$

$$s = \sqrt{s^2}$$

$$s = \sqrt{9} \qquad\qquad s = \sqrt{4}$$

$$= \underline{\underline{3}} \qquad\qquad = \underline{\underline{2}}$$

We will let these examples stand as a demonstration of the fact that formula (3.14) yields results that are equivalent to those obtained from the basic definition of the variance (3.12). To provide illustrations of (3.14) with data more representative of that normally encountered in educational usage, we will apply it to the height and spelling data of Tables 3 and 4. As can be seen from these applications, it makes no difference where zero in the d scale is assigned, or what the value of i is in the original distribution, so long as the d scale is organized in unit (..., −3, −2, −1, 0, 1, 2, 3, ...) steps.

Distribution of Ten Children's Heights

X	f	d	fd	fd²
70	1	3	3	9
65	2	2	4	8
60	4	1	4	4
55	2	0	0	0
50	1	−1	−1	1
	N = 10		$\Sigma fd = 10$	$\Sigma fd^2 = 22$

Distribution of Forty-eight Children's Spelling Scores

X	f	d	fd	fd²
51	1	6	6	36
48	1	5	5	25
45	4	4	16	64
42	5	3	15	45
39	9	2	18	36
36	11	1	11	11
33	8	0	0	0
30	3	−1	−3	3
27	2	−2	−4	8
24	2	−3	−6	18
21	2	−4	−8	32
	N = 48		$\Sigma fd = 50$	$\Sigma fd^2 = 278$

$$s^2 = i^2 \left[\frac{\Sigma fd^2}{N} - \left(\frac{\Sigma fd}{N} \right)^2 \right] \tag{3.14}$$

$$s^2 = 5^2 \left[\frac{22}{10} - \left(\frac{10}{10} \right)^2 \right] \qquad s^2 = 3^2 \left[\frac{278}{48} - \left(\frac{50}{48} \right)^2 \right]$$

$$= 25 \,[2.2 - 1] \qquad\qquad = 9 \,[5.79 - 1.09]$$

$$= 25 \,[1.2] \qquad\qquad\quad = 9 \,[4.7]$$

$$= \underline{30} \qquad\qquad\qquad\quad = \underline{42.3}$$

$$s = \sqrt{30} \qquad\qquad\qquad s = \sqrt{42.3}$$

$$= \underline{\underline{5.48}} \qquad\qquad\qquad\quad = \underline{\underline{6.50}}$$

The process of extracting square roots, as required for s, is a problem to some students. Several procedures for determining square roots are available in elementary algebra and other mathematics textbooks. Reasonably close approximations can be found by using commonly available tables of squares and square roots.

A full appreciation of the meaning and importance of s^2 and s cannot be gained in this short discussion. Their value as descriptive statistical indices of variation and as a method for their computation can be established, however. The most direct and simple means for interpreting either s^2 or s is as a comparative statistic. For example, as we have seen in the illustrations used, the four children who were timed in solving an arithmetic problem were less variable in terms of time required the second time than they were the first time, as is indicated by the standard deviations of 2 and 3. Beyond this interpretation, the values of s^2 and s will not only be a function of the variability of measures but also the values of the measures, just as is the case with means. As we use s^2 and s to describe phenomena, we acquire a "feel" for their expected values in terms of usage.

Standard Scores

Over the years, psychometricians have developed a number of kinds of standard scores which have found their way into educational measurement. By standard score, we mean score scales with standard meaning in the face of the great variety of raw scores used. One way, but by no means the only way, to provide standard scales is to "fix" the scales so that they have common means and standard deviations. The most fundamental score of this nature is called z and is defined as:

$$z = \frac{X - \overline{X}}{s}, \text{ where} \tag{3.15}$$

X is the raw score to be transformed to z
$\overline{X}$ is the mean of the X score distribution
s is the standard deviation of the X score distribution.

To transform raw scores to z-scores, the mean and standard deviation must be available. Given these statistics, determining z is then a straightforward application of (3.15). For example, given scores of 18, 16, 15, 13, 10, . . . from a distribution with $\overline{X} = 15$ and $s = 5$, the equivalent z scores are: $\frac{18 - 15}{5} = 0.6, \frac{16 - 15}{5} = 0.2, \frac{15 - 15}{5} = 0.0,$ $\frac{13 - 15}{5} = -0.4,$ and $\frac{10 - 15}{5} = -1.0, \ldots$ From the definition of z, it can be shown that the mean of *every* distribution *of z-scores* is zero, and its standard deviation 1.0. These facts allow the immediate interpretation of any z-score in terms of position within the distribution. That is, we know right away whether a given z is above or below its mean by its albegraic sign. Further, we know how many standard deviations it is in reference to its mean, as z is by definition the deviation of a score from its mean in units of its standard deviation.

Certain other kinds of standard scores are derivations of z. For example, a score known as T is defined as:

$$T = 10z + 50 \qquad (3.16)$$

To convert scores to T requires first a transformation to z, and then the application of formula (3.16). All such T score distributions have a mean of 50 and $s = 10$. These facts, again, allow the quick interpretation of given T scores. For example, a T score of 70 would indicate performance two standard deviations above the mean.

A number of Educational Testing Services tests (Graduate Record Examination, College Boards, and others) utilize a standard score defined as:

$$C.E.E.B. \text{ score} = 100z + 500 \qquad (3.17)$$

It follows that this type of score distribution has a mean of 500 and $s = 100$. Again, knowing these characteristics allows the quick interpretation of such standard scores in terms of their position within their distribution.

If we know something about the shape of a distribution or are willing to assume some type of distribution, then further interpretations of standard scores may be made involving their percentile ranks. The most common illustration of this is the employment of the normal curve. By referring back to Figure 7, we can see that, essentially, the scale given directly beneath the curve is a z-scale. By assumption that whatever is being measured is normally distributed, conversions from z or T or C.E.E.B. or I.Q., and so forth, can be made to the appropriate percentile rank (cumulative percentages) dictated by the curve. If a distribution is *not* normally distributed, it follows that such conversions are invalid.

Relationships

It is said that we live in a world of cause and effect. This viewpoint holds that nothing occurs by chance even though full and complete explanations may be lacking. In this sense, there is a great difference between ignorance and capriciousness. The scientist's basic purpose is to try to discover the relationships among natural phenomena in order to understand them more fully if not to control them. This doctrine of science is, in the minds of many, applicable to social and educational problems. The philosophical school of thought upon which their position rests is called naturalism. Most educational practice is based upon this position, but frequently in demonstration, remains at an assumptive level. The empiricist asks for observable evidence which supports the logical arguments of the naturalist. In the quest for supporting evidence, statisticians have developed a number of techniques designed to describe the relationship between variables. Those techniques result in indices of relationship which are abstractions. As such, they are subject to misuse and abuse as are any other statistical indices. It will be our purpose to try to establish conceptual meaning for this general class of statistics and to point out some common interpretive pitfalls. Computational skill, although important, is secondary to these general purposes.

Let us define a *variable* as any trait which may be possessed in varying amounts by different individuals. Intelligence, spelling ability, computational skill, and many other educational or psychological traits are examples. It is obvious that educational variables are relatively complex and that they are frequently interrelated. That is, variables may be associated, or interdependent, or contingent one with another, and frequently in complex ways. For example, we might say that precipitation is a function of (related to) humidity. However, it would be more accurate to say that precipitation is a function of humidity, temperature, air pressure, and perhaps other variables about which we know little. Analogously, we may say that learning is a function of intelligence, but to be more precise, we might wish to add other variables such as age, past experience, motivation, interest, and so on. The point is that it is easy to oversimplify complex relationships in educational contexts. Human performance is seldom a simple matter of determining direct one-to-one correspondence between variables, no matter how much we would like this to be the case. *Correlations* are important indices of relationships between variables. One of their fundamental uses is to discover not only how one variable accounts for (is related to) another variable, but also the degree to which they do not account for each other. Correlational analyses can be complex, involving many variables often interrelated in complicated ways. Such analyses are beyond the scope of this discussion, but an awareness of them is appropriate as an antidote to superficial explanations of educational problems.

In educational measurement, the use of correlation coefficients is important at a fundamental level in two crucial concepts, namely, validity and reliability. More will be said of these concepts in a later chapter. For now, let us simply deal with some of the logic and mechanics of correlation itself.

The Pearson Correlation Coefficient

It may be recalled that Karl Pearson, a student of Sir Francis Galton, developed some of the early correlational methodology. One of the most basic indices of relationship is called, after its originator, the Pearson product-moment correlation coefficient. It bears the simpler symbolic designation r and was originally defined as:

$$r = \frac{\Sigma z_1 \, z_2}{N}, \text{ where} \tag{3.18}$$

z_1 is a given person's measure in a variable (1) in standard score form;

z_2 is the same person's measure in the second variable (2) in standard score form;

$\Sigma z_1 z_2$ is the sum of the products of these standard scores for a set of individuals;

N   is the number of pairs of observations or the number of persons each of whom has a measure 1 and a measure 2.

Although not directly apparent from the formula itself, it can be shown that the limits for values of r are $+1.00$ and -1.00, with the possibility of any intermediate value including zero. If we consider this basic definition (3.18) for a moment, it will add to our understanding of r. It may be recalled that, when measures are transformed to z-scores, they may take either positive or negative values, depending upon their position in respect to their mean. It follows that, if in a given set of measures, the individuals rank in identical order in each of two variables, the highest possible value of $\Sigma z_1 z_2$ will obtain (recall that the product of two negative factors is positive). In this situation, we would say that there is a perfect positive relationship or association between the variables. When this is the case, mathematically $\Sigma z_1 z_2 = N$, and $r = \frac{N}{N}$ or 1. To contrast this, let us suppose that ranks in the one variable are perfectly inversely related to ranks in the other variable. That is, the highest individual on measure 1 is lowest on measure 2, the next highest on 1 is next to the lowest on 2, and so on. In this situation, every positive z_1 is associated with a negative z_2 and vice versa. Thus, the value of $\Sigma z_1 z_2$ is negative and its absolute value a maximum. This situation would describe a perfect inverse relationship between the variables, or as could be shown, $\Sigma z_1 z_2 = -N$ and $r = \frac{-N}{N} = -1.00$. Again to contrast this situation, let us suppose that there were no relationship between ranks on the one variable and ranks on the other. The ways that z_1 and z_2 would then be associated would be a matter of chance, with some values of $z_1 z_2$ being positive and some negative. In this situation, the value for $\Sigma z_1 z_2$ would tend toward zero, as would the value for r. From this discussion, it should be apparent that the index of association, r, reflects the degree to which measures in two variables are related. Table 11 contains a summary of the values of r and verbal statements suggesting, in general, the strength of association the various values of r represent. Obviously, the meaning given to any particular correlation coefficient will depend upon the particular context, but Table 11 does provide rough guidelines for interpretation.

The definition of r provided by formula (3.18) requires that the measures in each variable be in standard score (z) form. This is an unrealistic requirement since our interest is usually in the distributions

TABLE 11

General Verbal Statements Suggesting the Strength of Association between Variables Represented by Various Values of r

Values of r	Strength of Association
1.00	Perfect, positive
.80 to .99	Strong, direct
.60 to .79	Moderate, direct
.40 to .59	Slight, direct
.20 to .39	Weak but positive
- .20 to .20	Weak to chance
- .40 to -.21	Weak but negative
- .60 to -.41	Slight, inverse
- .80 to -.61	Moderate, inverse
- .99 to -.81	Strong, inverse
-1.00	Perfect, inverse

of original measures. Formula (3.18) has been transformed mathematically into a number of equivalent expressions. A useful computational formula for r is:

$$r = \frac{\frac{\Sigma X_1 X_2}{N} - \bar{X}_1 \bar{X}_2}{s_1 s_2}, \text{ where} \qquad (3.19)$$

$\Sigma X_1 X_2$ is the sum of the products of the two variables for all individuals.

N   is the number of individuals having measures in X_1 and X_2.

$\bar{X}_1$ is the mean of the first variable.

$\bar{X}_2$ is the mean of the second variable.

s_1 is the standard deviation of the first variable.

s_2 is the standard deviation of the second variable.

Formula (3.19) has been selected here as a computational model for r because it utilizes the means and standard deviations of each variable—

desirable statistics for describing each variable in its own right—and requires only the single $X_1 X_2$ cross-product term.

To illustrate the use of formula (3.19), let us suppose that we have for each of ten pupils, measures obtained from two classroom tests in arithmetic. Let Test 1 be the first variable, representing a test designed to assess the ability to perform arithmetic operations with fractions and mixed numbers. Let Test 2 be the second variable, representing a test designed to assess the ability to perform arithmetic operations with decimal fractions. We might, at this point, hypothesize that there will be a positive relationship between these measured abilities because they both include arithmetic operations and probably other "common" elements. We probably would not expect the relationship to be perfect since there may be distinctive features, as well as some error associated with the measurement of each ability. The data and application of (3.19) are presented in Table 12.

TABLE 12

Computational Illustration for Correlation Coefficient (r)

	Measure from Test on:			Distributions Reorganized for Computation of Standard Deviations									
Pupil	Fractions (X_1)	Decimals (X_2)	$X_1 X_2$	X_1	f	d	fd	fd^2	X_2	f	d	fd	fd^2
A	30	29	870	30	1	5	5	25	29	1	6	6	36
B	26	27	702	29	1	4	4	16	28	1	5	5	25
C	29	26	754	28	1	3	3	9	27	1	4	4	16
D	26	28	728	27	0	2	0	0	26	1	3	3	9
E	25	20	500	26	2	1	2	2	25	0	2	0	0
F	25	24	600	25	2	0	0	0	24	2	1	2	2
G	28	21	588	24	0	-1	0	0	23	1	0	0	0
H	23	23	529	23	1	-2	-2	4	22	0	-1	0	0
I	22	24	528	22	1	-3	-3	9	21	1	-2	-2	4
J	20	17	340	21	0	-4	0	0	20	1	-3	-3	9
Sums	$\Sigma X_1 = 254$	$\Sigma X_2 = 239$	$\Sigma X_1 X_2 = 6139$	20	1	-5	-5	25	19	0	-4	0	0
Means	$\bar X_1 = 25.4$	$\bar X_2 = 23.9$	$\dfrac{\Sigma X_1 X_2}{N} = 613.9$			$\Sigma fd = 14\text{-}10$	$\Sigma fd^2 = 90$		18	0	-5	0	0
						$= 4$			17	1	-6	-6	36
											$\Sigma fd = 20\text{-}11$	$\Sigma fd^2 = 137$
												$= 9$	

$$r = \frac{\dfrac{\Sigma X_1 X_2}{N} - \bar X_1 \bar X_2}{s_1 s_2} \quad (3.19)$$

$$r = \frac{613.9 - (25.4)(23.9)}{(2.97)(3.59)}$$

$$= \frac{613.9 - 607.1}{10.66} = \frac{6.8}{10.66}$$

$$= 0.64$$

$$s_1^2 = 1^2\left[\frac{90}{10} - \left(\frac{4}{10}\right)^2\right] \qquad s^2 = i^2\left[\frac{\Sigma fd^2}{N} - \left(\frac{\Sigma fd}{N}\right)^2\right] \quad (3.13)$$

$$= 1[9 - .16]$$

$$= 8.84$$

$$s_1 = \sqrt{8.84}$$

$$s_1 = 2.97$$

$$s_2^2 = 1^2\left[\frac{137}{10} - \left(\frac{9}{10}\right)^2\right]$$

$$= 1[13.7 - .81]$$

$$= 12.89$$

$$s_2 = \sqrt{12.89}$$

$$s_2 = 3.59$$

Rho (ρ)

Another, and simpler, formula for estimating correlation coefficients is based upon the ranks of the measures of each variable when each is ranked separately. This coefficient is called *rho* and is symbolized by that Greek letter (ρ) in order to distinguish it from *r*. The two coefficients are not equivalent, but, under many conditions, are quite similar.

The relative simplicity of determining rho justifies its use where approximations of r are acceptable. The formula for rho is:

$$\rho = 1 - \frac{6\Sigma d^2}{N(N^2-1)}, \text{ where} \qquad (3.20)$$

d^2 is the square of the differences between ranks in each variable for an individual.

Σd^2 is the sum of such squared differences for all individuals.

N   is the number of individuals each having measures in the two variables.

Table 13 provides an illustration of the application of formula (3.20) to the same data that were presented in Table 12. The first two columns reproduce the raw scores given in Table 12. The next two columns are a conversion of the original measures to ranks. As can be seen, X_1 for individual A is 30 which has the rank 1 in the variable X_1. Individual B's X_1 of 26 is a tied rank with D; therefore, the ranks these two scores occupy, fourth and fifth, are averaged and assigned to both 26's. (Tied ranks are always averaged among the number of ties, and the ranks used to obtain the average are then discarded. Here there are two 26's which use ranks 4 and 5, and so the next lower score proceeds to rank 6, etc.) C's score of 29 takes rank 2, and so on through the X_1 distribution. The X_2 measures are then ranked within their distribution. The column headed d is the difference between ranks, disregarding the algebraic signs. Finally, the d^2 column is the square of each difference between ranks. After the d^2 values are summed, then formula (3.20) is applied, as in Table 13. As can be seen, the obtained value for ρ in this situation is 0.65 which is virtually the same as the earlier $r = 0.64$. Again, it should be recognized that, as the ranks for an individual are similar in both variables, d and d^2 will take minimum values, Σd^2 will approach zero, and $\rho = 1 - \frac{6\Sigma d^2}{N(N^2-1)}$ will approach 1.00. Thus, those values near zero will indicate little if any relationship among the variables, and those values near 1.00 will indicate a high relationship among variables.

Interpretation of Correlations

Let us now consider, in a more general sense, some conditions common in educational contexts, conditions which influence the relationships among variables. That is, we will consider certain common conditions which will influence the magnitude and/or meaning of the coefficients of correlation we encounter.

The first thing to recognize is that a coefficient by itself does not prove anything about the meaning of the relationship among variables. A common temptation is to impute causality to relationships described

TABLE 13

Computational Illustration of Rank Difference Coefficient
of Correlation, Rho

	Raw Scores		Ranks for			
Individual	X_1	X_2	X_1	X_2	d	d^2
A	30	29	1	1	0.0	0.00
B	26	27	4.5	3	1.5	2.25
C	29	26	2	4	2.0	4.00
D	26	28	4.5	2	2.5	6.25
E	25	20	6.5	9	2.5	6.25
F	25	24	6.5	5.5	1.0	1.00
G	28	21	3	8	5.0	25.00
H	23	23	8	7	1.0	1.00
I	22	24	9	5.5	3.5	12.25
J	20	17	10	10	0.0	0.00

$$\Sigma d^2 = 58.00$$

$$\rho = 1 - \frac{6\Sigma d^2}{N(N^2-1)}$$

$$= 1 - \frac{6(58)}{10(10^2-1)}$$

$$= 1 - \frac{348}{990}$$

$$= 1 - .35$$

$$= .65$$

by r. Given a high r, we are tempted to say X_1 causes X_2. Carefully constructed experiments may lend support to the notion of cause and effect but seldom, if ever, prove it. It is well to remember that r, by itself, is simply a description. It describes the way the measures in two variables happen to be associated for a particular sample of data available at a particular time under particular conditions. In the illustration we have used in this section, should we say X_1 (arithmetic test score representing ability to perform operations with fractions and mixed numbers) causes X_2 (score representing ability to perform operations with decimal fractions) on the basis of $r = 0.64$? Or does X_2 cause X_1? In any case, we must recognize that the obtained r represents the degree of association for a specific set of pupils obtained from specific tests under unique conditions. Beyond that, other variables such as general intelligence, general arithmetic ability, cooperativeness, and other possibilities may be related to both X_1 and X_2. To conclude that X_1 causes X_2, then, would be an error. For example, it is said that the number of years spent in school are related to economic success. It is tempting for educators such as ourselves to conclude that the one causes the other. But who is likely to stay in school? If the answer is "the economically favored," then we may be flirting with a specious argument, in part. Let us think about the old saws such as "haste makes waste," "pride rideth before a fall," "many hands make light work," in this regard. We could end up with too many slow equalitarians if we take these old "truths" too literally. In the same way, we run the risk of imputing cause to variables which simply are tagging along empirically in educational situations. Human history is full of "theories" based upon no more than spurious associations.

Another common pitfall in the interpretation of r is due to a condition called *contamination*. Contamination means that the values assigned to the one variable are influenced by a knowledge of values of the other variable. A more blunt way to say it is that one measure biases the other, or that some general set biases them both. If blue eyes, blond hair, and clean finger nails result in certain kinds of influence upon X_1 and X_2 measures that are systematically different from the influence of the grubby, then r may be misleading. In situations where our judgment enters into the assignment of values to X_1 or X_2, it is difficult to avoid contamination. On the other hand, an overconcern regarding contamination can also result in misleading data. The best we can do, usually, is to recognize the possibility of contamination and try to account for it.

A third general condition which influences the meaning of correlation coefficients is the variability of the measures. This condition directly influences the size of r. It may be obvious that if all individuals had the same measure in either X_1 or X_2, r would be zero. To the degree that measures are constrained or truncated, r will be reduced. This condition may arise from insensitive (too gross) measures, homogeneous samples of individuals, or both factors simultaneously. It should be apparent on this basis that r can never be adequately interpreted without due consideration of what X_1 and X_2 are and how they were obtained, as well as consideration of the nature of the group upon which the data is established.

The reliability of the measures (X_1 and X_2) also influences correlation coefficients. Reliability will be treated more fully later, but let us consider it to be related to error of measurement. To the degree that chance error is reflected in the measures of either variable, the correlation coefficient will be reduced. Other things being equal, the more error-free each measure is, the more confidence we may place upon the obtained coefficient. The meaningfulness of this generalization will be more apparent after considering the concept of reliability.

Finally, where human characteristics are concerned, the size of correlation coefficients is likely to be a function of the amount of time between the obtaining of X_1 and X_2. People change, and change differentially. The longer the time span between X_1 and X_2, the more likely it is that conditions influencing ranks in the second variable will occur. Of course, if the purpose of an investigation is to estimate the relationship between variables over long time periods, then long time spans are appropriate. The problem is that people are not like the objects in experiments of the natural scientist. They are not subject to control in the same sense. Fate wanders in its influence without the approval of the social scientist or the educational researcher. To the degree that such influence operates differentially and is unknown, the meaning of r is unknown.

At this point, we may wonder if indices of relationship are ever worth the effort. Yes they are—but. . . As we append qualifying statements to them, we are, in fact, making interpretations, the *sine qua non* of evaluation.

ADDITIONAL READING

DIEDERICH, PAUL B. "No. 5. Shortcut Statistics for Teacher-Made Tests," *Evaluation and Advisory Series*. Princeton: Educational Testing Service, n.d.
  Pamphlet available free upon request from ETS. Provides a clear, concise review of procedures for the analysis of classroom tests.
EDWARDS, A. L. *Statistical Analysis*. rev. ed. New York: Holt, Rinehart & Winston, 1958.
  This book is clear and sound. It provides an excellent first reader in statistics, but contains material of interest to advanced readers as well.
LINDQUIST, E. F. *Statistical Analysis in Educational Research*. Boston: Houghton Mifflin Co., 1940.
  Old, but a classic "first course" statistics book oriented to education.
SCHOER, LOWELL A. *An Introduction to Statistics and Measurement: A Programmed Book*. Boston: Allyn & Bacon, 1964.
  Useful as a self-teaching device for learning the necessary statistics of classroom measurement.

4

Instructional Assessment
and Test Construction

Up to this point, we have considered something of the general context, purpose, history, philosophy, and method of evaluation in education. It is now our task to become somewhat more specific. To do this, we shall direct our attention in the two remaining chapters to methods for achieving some of the purposes of evaluation. Interpretive emphasis will be added to the discussions of technique and procedure for the purpose of orienting to tools as means of achieving ends and goals. Many of the necessary concepts and understandings for this task have been dealt with in the preceding chapters. It is now time to use them to further our grasp of educational evaluation.

Educational Systems: The Classroom and Beyond

Most fundamentally, the purpose of education is to effect change in students. In fact, all definitions of learning, in one way or another, should be framed in terms of changes in behavior. If we espouse effective learning in education, we necessarily conceive of the role of the teacher as a change agent. Some educators seem to be uncomfortable with this notion, claiming that children should be free to develop and grow with a minimum of influence from external sources. Such a position ignores the fact that pupils will be influenced by our concept of learning-teaching whatever it is. Our position is that behavioral changes in pupils are inevitable, and that it is the educators' responsibility to systematize instruction so as to achieve effective change consistent with the educational philosophy of the culture. In this view, teachers are engineers designing educational experiences for the most effective achievement of objectives possible. Like engineers, they are not expected to be infallible nor to ignore practical reality, but they are expected to be competent in dealing with a wide range of factors influencing instructional programs. Further, teachers should be able to deal with instructional "design" in terms of the abstractions, principles, and theories of their profession. This is the distinction between the engineer and the mechanic. What this suggests regarding pupil change is that such change will be specified, controlled, and monitored. As is usually the case, our conceptualizations as to ways of doing these things are oversimplified, but such oversimplification is necessary in order to deal with the process at an abstract level.

A model of the instructional process has been developed by Glaser[1] and is shown in Figure 10. As has been suggested, the model is obviously simplified in that each of the elements (A, B, C, D) is itself complex. The model does suggest, however, that to consider the element C alone as the

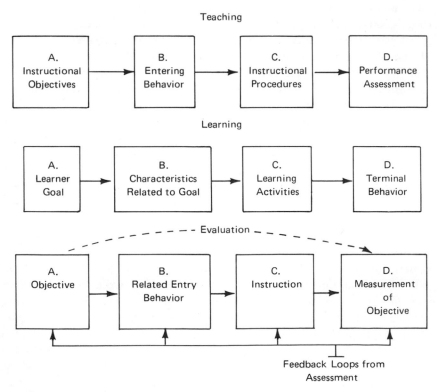

Figure 10. Model of an Instructional System with Parallel Teaching, Learning, and Evaluation Paths.

---

[1]Adapted from Robert Glaser, "Psychology and Instructional Technology," in *Training Research and Education,* ed. R. Glaser, (Pittsburgh: University of Pittsburgh Press, 1962), p. 6.

complete teaching or learning situation is a seriously limited view of instruction. The last line—the evaluation path—is an attempt to conceptualize instruction in its more dynamic state. Here it is held that we begin with an objective, (A), (or objectives). A is assumed to be rationally established, consistent with the discussion in the first chapter. The broken arrow proceeding from A to D suggests that some kind of first estimate of the status of the learners has been made regarding the need to reach the objective; that is, the objective not only is important (logically established), but is unmet or needed (either assumed or empirically established). Behavior and characteristics of the learner, either known or believed to be related to the attainment of the objective, are then taken into account. Those experiences, skills, and other predispositions to the attainment of the objective which already characterize the learner are considered in the conduct of the instruction itself. The instructional element of the model consisting of those procedures utilized to attain the objective is thus a function of the preceding elements.

Lastly, performance assessment consisting of measurement procedure (tests, observations, ratings, etc.) provide estimates of the degree to which the objective has been attained. From information obtained in assessment, feedback loops to each of the three preceding elements are possible. In this model, it is apparent that measurement is essential to each of the other components of instruction. In fact, as information from assessment is fed back and used anywhere in the instructional system, evaluative judgments are being made. The figure should provide an indication of the crucial nature of objectives to the total system. For our purposes, it is important to note that statements of instructional objectives are as essential to assessment as they are to instruction, and that evaluation incorporates all three.

At the level of instruction and the assessment of its results, it is evident that specificity is required. Without such specificity on the instructional side, we will not know where we are going on the assessment side and, equally important, we will not know when we arrive. Therefore, the same reference point, the objective, is crucial to both. Because of this, we need to consider the development of statements of objectives. Many of the textbooks on testing and educational evaluation have emphasized the importance of specifying objectives and have offered suggestions for writing them. These suggestions can be summarized in two points stated by Lindvall[2]:

1. Statements of specific objectives should be worded in terms of the pupil.
2. Statements of specific objectives must include the exact behavior that the pupil is to be expected to exhibit.

---

[2]C. M. Lindvall, *Defining Educational Objectives.* (Pittsburgh: University of Pittsburgh Press, 1964), p. 4.

In support of the first point, it can be said that both instruction and evaluation must be pupil-centered. Learning objectives must be learner oriented and must avoid explicit reference to teacher activity, instructional media, and methods of communication lest they become the focal points of instruction. As for the second point, it demands that the manifestations of the objective—the pupil's ability to do something—is the only evidence admissible for assessing the attainment of the objective. For example, an understanding of a principle can only be known on the basis of an ability to explain it, use it, predict outcomes from it, and so forth, and not on the basis of testimonials for its existence.

It could be said that a meaningful objective is one that succeeds in communicating the instructional intent and that excludes alternatives to it. It is apparent that educators, in writing their objectives, use many words that are loaded with ambiguity. That is, they are open to a wide range of interpretation. In order to deal with this problem, Mager[3] suggests that clarity in describing terminal behavior (what the learner does) can be aided by:

1. identifying and naming the overall behavioral act;
2. defining the important conditions under which the behavior occurs, including the givens and/or restrictions and limitations; and
3. defining a criterion of acceptable performance.

A practical means of reaching these recommendations is to think of a statement of an instructional objective as a sentence having a subject, verb, and object. The subject must be the learner because he is the target of the instruction. Verbs which are action verbs conveying explicit behavior are preferred. For example, let us consider the following phrases, each of which is a verb infinitive:

Ambiguous	*Less Ambiguous*
to know, to understand, to *really* understand, to appreciate, to *fully* appreciate, to grasp the significance of, to enjoy, to believe, to have faith in, etc.	to write, to recite, to identify, to differentiate, to solve, to construct, to list, to compare, to contrast, to choose, to elect, etc.

The intent of these samples is to illustrate that explicit action verbs are less ambiguous than verbs denoting inner behavior and mental states, such as understanding or appreciation, because they lead to observable acts. Finally, the object of the sentence will specify what is to be acted upon and under what conditions. In a sense, it specifies content, that is, what is read, recited, solved, chosen, and so on, and it defines the important conditions under which the behavior is to occur.

---

[3]Robert F. Mager, *Preparing Objectives for Programmed Instruction.* (Palo Alto: Fearon Publishers, 1962).

From the preceeding discussion, it may be apparent that the gaining of specificity through instructional objectives has its price. Such objectives can suffer from too much specification and lead to trivial multiplicity. In the final analysis, judgments regarding that point can be made only by those holding the responsibility for instruction and by their peers. The cost of not specifying instructional objectives seems to be even greater to both the conduct and the evaluation of that instruction.

Variables in Instruction

Educators, of course, deal with pupil learning and development. Their purpose is to direct desirable change in efficient ways so as to enable the recipients of instruction to achieve maximum capability. It should also be emphasized that pupil development is influenced by a number of potent learning forces external to the school. Such forces include the home and family, the peer culture, and other individuals and institutions within the general culture. In addition, there are biological, intellectual, and emotional predeterminants to achievement within the individual himself. That we do not fully understand these factors is attested to by the ever-recurrent "nature-nurture" controversies over theories of human development.

The fact remains, however, that educators must deal with pupils' behavior which is at once complex and confounded by influences from a number of sources. No simple solution to the dilemma presented by this complexity is possible; but by categorizing the various pupil behaviors that are of interest to educators, we may be able better to conceptualize the evaluation problem. It would appear that pupils' behaviors which are of interest as instructional objectives occur in four general systems, namely: intellectual, emotional, physical-motor, and social. These general systems will be discussed in turn.

Intellectual Objectives

School learning has traditionally been concerned with intellectual behavior and its development. That is, schools have given, and still do give, highest priority to the learning of skills associated with communication in the various disciplines. Tasks associated with speaking, reading, and writing form the basic objectives of most instructional programs. In the primary and elementary years, these behaviors are especially associated with the mother tongue. Other special "languages" such as mathematics, the various sciences, social studies, and so on are added and elaborated upon at such times as deemed efficient by curriculum specialists. But in dealing intellectually with the concepts and principles of any discipline, it has been held by many that there are processes of thinking which are more fundamental than the content itself. Bloom's *Taxonomy*[4] is an example of this viewpoint.

The taxonomy itself is a system of classifying educational objectives in terms of the cognitive behaviors of the learners. The classes of behavior are arranged in hierarchical order, that is, in behaviors considered to be ordered from simple to complex. This is an important feature to consider, as it illustrates the fact that both instruction and its evaluation involve more than the knowledge of facts. Two broad categories of behavior are included, (1) knowledge and (2) intellectual abilities and skills. The first category consists of one class of behavior; the second consists of six classes. The various major classes are listed, defined, and illustrated in Table 14. The importance of the taxonomy for us is that it illustrates the hierarchical nature of intellectual behavior, and it underscores the fact that neither instruction nor assessment should be "stuck" exclusively at the level of factual details, as many critics charge is the case.

Emotional Objectives

It has probably struck the reader, perhaps many times, that all of the objectives of education are not intellectual, and that those which are, are not exclusively intellectual. Mental behavior has its emotional components, a fact supported by both experience and learning research. Teachers and educators are interested in how pupils feel about themselves and their environment, both because feelings are important by themselves and because they influence all behavior. Objectives of this sort have been called *affective* and are defined in general as those objectives which deal with feeling and emotive behavior. These objectives include interests, attitudes, appreciations, and values. Krathwohl et al.[5] have devised a taxonomy for the affective domain of behavior. The principle upon which this taxonomy was devised is the degree to which the pupil has internalized the affective objectives. Table 15 follows the form of Table 14 in presenting the various classes, their definitions, and examples. Again, the importance of this taxonomy is not so much its particular classifications as it is the recognition that affective behaviors constitute important, legitimate educational objectives and are themselves complex.

Physical-Motor and Social Objectives

Two additional general classes of behavior should be mentioned in connection with educational objectives. They are physical-motor and

---

[4]Benjamin S. Bloom et al., *Taxonomy of Educational Objectives: Handbook I: Cognitive Domain* (New York: David McKay Co., 1956).

[5]D. R. Krathwohl, B. S. Bloom, and B. B. Masia, *Taxonomy of Objectives: The Classification of Educational Goals. Handbook II: Affective Domain* (New York: David McKay Co., 1964).

TABLE 14

Classes of Intellectual Behavior, Definitions, and Examples from Bloom's
*Taxonomy of Educational Objectives**

Class of Behavior	Definition	Examples
I.		
1. Knowledge	Includes behaviors and situations emphasizing remembering through recognition or recall of ideas, material, terms, facts, conventions, methodology, principles, and generalizations.	Recall of specific information, definitions, symbols, or procedures. Knowledge of organizing, judging or criticizing. Knowledge of major ideas, schemes, and theories.
II. Abilities and Skills		
2. Comprehension	Includes behaviors which represent an understanding of the literal message contained in either symbolic or situational communication.	Translation between levels of abstraction, symbolic or verbal forms. Interpretation of communications into major ideas and their interrelationships. Extension or extrapolation to determine implications and consequences.
3. Application	Requires the use of comprehension (abstractions) in particular situations.	Ability to relate social principles to current events. Ability to apply mathematical principles to practical problems. Ability to apply scientific abstractions to new or novel situations.
4. Analysis	Emphasizes the breakdown of material into parts and determining organization by detection of interrelationship among parts.	Ability to detect assumptions. Ability to detect fallacies, supportive statements, relevant and irrelevant statements to an argument. Ability to recognize form, pattern, and organization of material.
5. Synthesis	Organizes parts and elements to form a whole— a pattern or structure not there before.	Skill in writing by following developing organization. Ability to describe effectively or to make a speech. Ability to plan an experiment or devise tests of hypotheses. Ability to design tools or other objects. Ability to theorize. Ability to discover and generalize mathematical concepts.
6. Evaluation	Makes judgments toward some end about the value of ideas, methods, or materials.	Ability to apply internal standards as criteria. Ability to apply external and comparative standards as criteria. Ability to apply aesthetic standards as criteria.

*Benjamin S. Bloom, Max D. Englehart, Edward J. Furst, Walker H. Hill, and David R. Krathwohl, *Taxonomy of Educational Objectives: Handbook I: Cognitive Domain*, 1956. Adapted by permission of David McKay Co., Inc., New York.

TABLE 15

Classes of Affective Behavior, Definitions, and Examples from Krathwohl's
Taxonomy of Educational Objectives *

Class of Behavior	Definition	Examples
1. Receiving (Attending)	A willingness to receive or attend to phenomena and stimuli. Proceeds from awareness, to willingness, to selection.	Is aware of aesthetic factors in learning and life. Accepts ethnic and cultural differences. Listens to and appreciates divergent views. Is alert to various types of voluntary reading.
2. Responding	Responses going beyond attending, to *active* attending, to phenomena and stimuli.	Obeys rules and regulations. Is willing to participate. Voluntarily reads, studies, and participates. Finds pleasure and enjoyment in activities.
3. Valuing	Holding that things, phenomena, or behaviors have worth.	Desires to develop abilities. Demonstrates a sense of responsibility for others' welfare. Examines various positions on issues for the purpose of forming an opinion. Is devoted to ideas and ideals.
4. Organization	Involving the organization of several values into a system.	Relates ethical standards and goals to others. Organizes the assumptions associated with codes of conduct and systems of faith. Weighs social policies and practices against the general welfare.
5. Characterization by a value (or value complex).	Characterization of a person's behavior by his value system—internalization of the values he holds.	Views problems in objective and realistic terms with tolerance. Has confidence in abilities. Develops a code of conduct and a life philosophy.

*David R. Krathwohl, Benjamin S. Bloom, and Bertram B. Masia, *Taxonomy of Educational Objectives: Handbook II: Affective Domain,* 1964. Adapted by permission of David McKay Co., Inc., New York.

social behaviors. At this time, taxonomies for these domains are not available, although work is being done on the first. It would seem that many of the objectives of courses and programs involving performance and activity lend themselves readily to physical behaviors and coordination. In addition, many skills appear to be combinations of physical and mental acts. Music, art, driving, physical education, industrial arts, provide illustrations. Also, primary education's objectives suggest that a taxonomy could be built for social behavior. That working, playing, thinking, and planning are social activities is self-evident. The dynamics of groups from small to large offer rich material for the devising of educational experiences, not only at primary levels but in all school programs.

Again, our purpose here is to suggest some of the breadth and depth of educational objectives. It follows that if instruction is richly diverse, the same should be true of evaluation. Evaluative data tied to trivia, such as memory for facts, alone represents hopeless naïveté regarding education.

Test Formats and Measurement

It is not surprising, considering the diversity of educational purposes, that a large number of measurement forms have evolved. We shall call these various measurement procedures "test formats." Several kinds, particularly those which educators find useful for classroom application, will be discussed.

By far the largest share of assessment in classroom contexts involves tests constructed for the measurement of cognitive objectives. Such tests are properly held to be achievement tests and often provide the basis upon which evaluative decisions are made. These tests are usually paper-pencil exercises in which the pupil is given standard cues in the form of questions or statements. Once cued, the pupil is expected to respond in terms of his achievement either by providing an original response or by making a choice among responses already provided. The behavior elicited by these kinds of tests may be considered to be verbal, but it should be appreciated that verbal behavior is not necessarily simple or irrelevant. As can be understood from studying sources such as Bloom's *Taxonomy*, verbal behavior is cognitive and can be very complex. Further, verbal behavior is most relevant to the major portion of educational objectives. The point is that there is nothing inherently irrelevant or simple about paper-pencil tests, as some would hold. The quality of these tests is a matter of content, planning, and construction and represents the most valid data available for many purposes. Several types of paper-pencil tests are available, each offering its own advantages and disadvantages.

It is common practice for measurement textbooks to classify tests as being either essay or objective. The distinction is relative when objectivity is defined as the degree of agreement between independent scorers. Another way to distinguish essay tests from objective tests is in terms of the nature of the pupil's response. It is said that, in essay tests, the examinee constructs or supplies the response, whereas in objective tests, he chooses among responses supplied by the test. Again, this is a relative distinction. Essay responses can be quite stereotyped, and the behavior preceding objective test choices *can* be quite original. In practice, the distinctions are, perhaps, more obvious, and we will treat the various formats as though they are distinct.

Essay Forms

The traditional essay test has the longest history of the various formats in educational usage and is possibly the commonest form today. We shall define an essay test as one requiring a written response to a standard cue, such as a question or a request for discussion. Further, the format requires an evaluator's judgment regarding the completeness and quality of the response, for scoring purposes. Such tests can range from requests for one sentence (sometimes even just a word or a phrase) to term-paper length responses. The dominant characteristics of these tests are that they (1) provide freedom to the respondent in constructing the response, and (2) require scorer judgment regarding the merit of the response. These characteristics at once indicate the major strength and weakness of the essay form. The relative freedom, even requirement, for pupil planning, developing, and producing a response is precisely the behavior called for by many objectives. At the same time, the freedom of the format creates problems in scoring because, obviously, each pupil's response will be unique. This fact means that, somehow, the scorer is required to make judgments about the quality of differing responses to standard cues. To the degree that the judge is inconsistent in applying his "standard" to the various responses, a source of measurement error which will influence the reliability of the measurement is introduced.

An additional disadvantage sometimes associated with essay tests is that they typically involve a relatively small number of questions. Consequently, in situations where tests are designed to cover a number of objectives, essay tests may be an inefficient format in terms of representing the objectives. The amount of time required for scoring essay responses is sometimes mentioned as a disadvantage which is offset by the advantage of speedy and easy test construction. These characteristics may be more apparent than real. Given a large group to be tested, most teachers would think differently about the problem than if the group were small. The apparent advantage of easy construction may also be quicksand when we remind ourselves that achievement tests should be consistent with instructional objectives. If the objectives are diverse and complex, quickly constructed essay test items run the risk of being relatively invalid. "Discuss the causes of World War II" is an item providing greater evidence of shabby test construction than of profundity. A few generalizations and recommendations regarding the construction and scoring of essay tests should be useful to users of the format.

The first step in the construction of essay tests should be to review the instructional objectives of the course or unit to be tested. This step can help to control two common faults in any type of test. First, it will eliminate or sharply reduce the number of unrelated and tangential questions. Second, it will, to some degree, control the "balance" of the test so that certain objectives are not seriously over-represented to the neglect of others. In this regard, the constructor should, furthermore, attempt to concentrate on important questions which truly require a demonstration of essential skills, understandings, or knowledge. One test of this criterion is the opinion of others who are knowledgeable in the same area of instruction. The same test (external opinion) should be applied to essay questions in terms of their "answerability." Does the question have a specific, determinable answer? Do other authorities agree? With experience, the essay item constructor will discover that these two questions have a greater probability of receiving affirmative answers when the essay task is defined completely and specifically. Of course, the purpose of specificity in directions is to reduce ambiguity without taking from the examinee the responsibility of responding.

The task of grading essays can be improved by following several practical procedures. A good test of the quality of a question, and one that is also useful in grading, is the construction of an "ideal" answer. Such an answer will incorporate major points, organization, nuances, or whatever elements are deemed significant. Once the answer is established as proof of the workability of the question, it provides a guide for grading the papers. Many teachers not only fail to grade essays with the aid of such a guide, but they also read an entire test paper which frequently contains many questions before they proceed to the next pupil's paper. This practice invites changing standards from question to question, but it is a practice that can easily be mitigated by grading all papers a question at a time.

Further control on the problems of grading can be gained by concealing the identity of papers. This practice is appropriate for all of us who suffer biases either of the halo or of the pitchfork variety. Teachers do not like to admit to holding personal preconceptions, but because they are human, it is not unlikely that they do. One procedure for concealing pupil identity is simply to use a test registration card with name and identification numbers for the test papers. Only after grading is the personal identity of the examinee determined for record keeping purposes. Finally, if it is feasible, independent grading of papers by other readers is helpful in order to assess the degree of error associated with scoring as revealed by inter-reader inconsistency. This procedure can be a very awakening experience for essay readers in terms of scoring reliability.

Completion Forms

Another common test format which provides a sort of bridge between essay and objective types is the completion test. In this format, statements are presented with missing words or phrases. The examinee's task is to complete the statement by filling in the appropriate missing elements. The format is like the essay in that the examinee supplies the response from memory or reasoning. At the same time, the format is somewhat like objective tests in that the scoring standards tend to be unambiguous. That they are not completely so can be illustrated by the following item. (We shall assume that the illustration is valid for a certain group in a particular context.)

$.02 and $.03 are_____?

It should be clear that $.05 is correct. Or is it clear? How about 5¢? Or a nickle? Five pennies are o.k. But what about 5? Or 5 "sense"? Or "money"? Again, unless the ground rules are understood, even completion items can be difficult to score. Beyond this, there is an unfortunate tendency for teachers to "lift" statements verbatim from textbooks or other sources and to string a great number of blanks together with prepositions. It is difficult to defend completion items when either the cues are so minimal that responding becomes a guessing game, or when the item does not assess a meaningful objective. Under some conditions, the format is useful and efficient. As usual, this is primarily a matter of controlling the construction of items with significant and meaningful objectives.

True-False Forms

The true-false test is a specific test format of a type which could be called dichotomous (divided into two parts). Such tests require either one of two understood responses to statements. The responses may be in various forms, such as: true-false, yes-no, + −, agree-disagree, or accept-reject. Fundamentally, the determination of truth or falsity is an important act in certain intellectual situations. For example, testing propositions and hypotheses, judging conclusions, evaluating extrapolations and relationships all tend to involve reductions to two-choice conclusions.

The problems of true-false tests center in their use rather than in any basic weakness. It is a difficult format to control, for several reasons. For one thing, there are very few statements outside of formal systems of logic which are inherently true. Most statements relating to instruction require qualification before they can be judged flatly as being true or false. This fact places the respondent, particularly the bright respondent, in a difficult quandary. He must ask himself if the statement is "true" enough to be true. There is usually no standard for making that judgment. Like the completion item, this form often is abused by lifting statements from textbooks or from other "authority." Such statements out of context are fertile ground for triviality. Minor changes, it is held, render the statement false. Memory for complete fidelity in reproduced statements is typically not considered among the more significant achievements of students.

In spite of these limitations, the format can be used with success when certain recommendations for item construction are followed. The foremost principle is to base the item upon matters of importance with respect to objectives. The items themselves must be precisely and definitely stated. Statements which combine more than one central idea should be avoided. Teachers should strive for items which may be defended rationally as being either true or false, but which are not so obvious as to be "give aways." Also to be avoided are specific determiners such as "often," "usually," "occasionally," which signal "true"; or "always," "never," "absolutely," "impossible," which signal "false." Practice has also shown that, if true-false tests are to achieve acceptable reliability, they need to be relatively long. The "pop quiz" of four to ten items is probably almost useless as a measuring device, in spite of any merit it may have for student motivation.

Multiple-Choice Forms

The multiple-choice test is, at the present time, probably the most widely used format. In this test, the examinee is presented with either a question or a statement to which a response is selected from among provided choices. The format is widely used by teachers and has been highly developed, especially by commercial test companies. The reasons for this probably lie in several natural advantages of the form. When well written, the multiple-choice item is very much like decision making in everyday life. That is, in many natural situations, we are faced with problems which require choosing a response from a number of alternatives. Our choices are usually based upon the best of several possibilities, and our task is to rule out alternatives containing faults. Also, the format simply requires a "best choice," not an absolute decision as in the true-false form. Finally, the format reduces, if not eliminates, the influence of scoring error as a function of scorer judgment, as is the case in essay testing. All of these advantages are not, of course, automatic. As with the other types of tests, certain recommendations for item writing are offered with the purpose of providing guides to better test construction.

As with all other forms, the cardinal requirement for constructing multiple-choice tests is that the items be written to assess the instructional objectives. In terms of their quality, they should address themselves to significant ideas, principles, or skills. Tinkelman[6] has offered a list of

---

[6]Sherman N. Tinkelman, *Readings in Measurement and Evaluation,* ed. Norman E. Grondlund (New York: Macmillan Co., 1968), Ch. 10.

technical recommendations for multiple-choice item writing, a list that summarizes important rules for their construction. His summary follows.

1. Is use of the direct question or incomplete statement form consistent with the most effective presentation of the individual items?
2. Are the items presented in clear and simple language, with vocabulary kept as simple as possible?
3. Does each item have one and only one correct answer?
4. Is each item concerned with a single central problem?
5. Is the central problem of each item stated clearly and completely in the stem?
6. Does the stem, so far as possible, include all words repeated in the responses?
7. Are negative statements avoided?
8. Is excessive "window dressing" avoided?
9. Do the responses or choices come at the ends of the incomplete statements?
10. Are the responses grammatically consistent with the stem and parallel with one another in form?
11. Are all responses plausible and attractive to pupils who lack the information or ability tested by the item?
12. Are the responses, so far as possible, arranged in numerical or logical order?
13. Are the responses independent and mutually exclusive?
14. Are the items free from extraneous clues due to grammatical inconsistencies, rote verbal associations, length of response, etc.?
15. Is the "none-of-these" option used only when appropriate?

The preceding discussion regarding test formats and recommendations for their construction is far from complete. There are many points which could be elaborated upon, as well as many which have been omitted. The serious student of test construction will wish to pursue some of the references provided here and go beyond to the vast literature available. The average teacher will, perhaps, find this discussion sufficient and will be willing to fight the measurement battle within the principles provided, using his own good sense. One further word of encouragement seems to be in order for that "typical" teacher. The word is "experiment." Test formats are subject to experimentation. The act of measurement requires every bit as much creative effort as does teaching itself. It also is as challenging and can be as rewarding. New forms should be tried. Fresh test items should be written. The game should be played as earnestly as the pupils deserve.

Finally, it appears to the writer that too many textbooks imply that the choice of test formats is restricted to paper-pencil forms. If we continue to reference our measurement procedures to our instructional objectives, it should be apparent that the products and performances of education are not always suited to paper-pencil testing. Art, music, physical education, industrial arts, driver training, and many other curricular divisions deal primarily with products and performances. Many of the objectives of the elementary school and of the so-called "academic" subjects likewise suggest concern for behaviors which may best be measured by other formats. Rating scales and observational checklists are possibly two under-used formats in education. If products and performances are elicited so that they are subject to comparison, that is, comparable, the use of scales and checklists is highly desirable. As in tests, the purpose of their use is to gain information which is valid for making distinctions among pupils in terms of the degree to which objectives have been met. In the final analysis, these devices are amazingly parallel to essay and multiple-choice formats and involve the same problems and promises.

Additional Reading

Bloom, Benjamin; Englehart, Max D.; Furst, Edward J.; Hill, Walker H.; and Krathwohl, David R. *Taxonomy of Educational Objectives—The Classification of Educational Goals, Handbook I: Cognitive Domain.* New York: David McKay Co., 1956.
  Assigns educational objectives to a taxonomy of behavior. It provides many excellent examples of items specifying those behaviors.
Buros, O. K. *The Sixth Mental Measurements Yearbook.* Highland Park, N. J.: Gryphon Press, 1965.
  Revised editions are available about every five years. These provide critical reviews of commercial tests. Comprehensive in terms of both reviews and coverage.
Ebel, Robert L. *Measuring Educational Achievement.* Englewood Cliffs, N. J.: Prentice-Hall, 1965.
  One of the best introductory books available on educational measurement. Material on test construction and analysis is outstanding.
Katz, Martin. "No. 4. Making the Classroom Test: A Guide for Teachers," *Evaluation and Advisory Series.* Princeton: Educational Testing Service, n.d.
  Pamphlet available free upon request from ETS. Handy and useful in guiding the teacher through the construction of classroom tests.
Mager, Robert F. *Preparing Objectives for Programmed Instruction.* Palo Alto: Fearon Publishers, 1962.
  Uses programmed learning to help teachers learn to prepare instructional objectives. The principles set forth are valid for nonprogrammed material as well.

5

Validity and Reliability

The evaluation of educational objectives is usually, if not always, based upon indirect measurement. We seldom directly see the results of instruction and learning. Rather, we accept as evidence of learning those behaviors that are held to be consistent with that learning. This fact ultimately means that the validity of the measures we use as evidence comes into question. It is neither obvious nor logical, on the face of it, that an I. Q. score is intelligence, or that a test score is achievement. Validity in measurement refers to the *degree* to which measures are meaningful representations of the traits they are designed to stand for. When we consider educational traits which are important and the measures used to represent them, we can see that validity is a crucial concept in evaluation. We can and often do attend to the wrong data in human affairs.

Beyond their validity, the measures we use are often not precise. One way to illustrate their imprecision is to note that independent but comparable measures of the same thing are inconsistent. If we hold that an object measured is constant, it follows that inconsistency between independent measures of it is caused by error. The reliability of measures refers to the precision of the measurement procedure or its freedom from error. These two concepts, validity and reliability, may be treated at both theoretical and practical levels. In either case, the reader can appreciate the fact that they are not independent concepts but that they influence each other. This final chapter deals with the validity and reliability of classroom and standardized tests. It also discusses at a practical level some of the procedures the reader may follow to estimate and control each.

Standardized Tests

We shall consider standardized tests to mean those tests which are available in complete form from some source external to the situation in which they are employed. They usually have norms to aid interpretation, as well as some technical information regarding their quality. Such tests are commonly purchased from publishers and sometimes include scoring service and materials designed to provide meaningful reports to pupils and teachers. As attractive as all these features are, it is still essential that users consider the evidence for any test's validity and reliability in order to be able to understand the data generated from the test.

Several sources of information about standardized tests will be useful as references. Probably the most comprehensive single source of this type is a series entitled *Mental Measurements Yearbooks*.[1] These yearbooks, under the editorship of O. K. Buros, have been published periodically and cover the major standardized tests of interest to educators. In addition to being an excellent bibliographical source for tests, the yearbook provides critical reviews by test experts. Certain journals contain abstracts and reviews of tests, and these are also useful. Journals which often report this kind of information are *Psychological Abstracts, Educational and Psychological Measurement, Journal of Counseling Psychology, Personnel and Guidance Journal,* and the *Review of Educational Research.* General guides for the evaluation of any educational or psychological test are provided by a manual entitled *Standards for Educational and Psychological Tests and Manuals*.[2]

The most specific information available regarding particular tests is that found in the manuals written for each test. Usually, specimen sets are available for tests at a nominal fee and include the test itself, an administrative manual, and a technical manual. Publishers catalogs provide information on the availability of these sets. The sources of information suggested here vary from reviews and reports about tests, to general guidelines for the conduct of one's own review, to specific descriptive information for particular tests. In all cases, some general knowledge of both validity and reliability will be required in order that the consumer will understand the information provided. For this reason, we will now consider some of the technical aspects of validity and reliability.

Validities

After verbally defining validity, there remains the problem of operationalizing the definition by specifying the evidence for it. When psy-

---

[1]O. K. Buros, *The Sixth Mental Measurements Yearbook* (Highland Park, N.J.: Gryphon Press, 1965).

[2]*Standards for Educational and Psychological Tests and Manuals* (Washington, D.C.: American Psychological Association, 1966).

chometricians operationalize, they point to the techniques and procedures used to gain the evidence. It is as though we would define the word "clock" by describing in detail the parts used to make a clock. There are several ways to so define validity. We shall consider three general classes, namely: content validity, criterion-related validity, and experimental validity.

Content validity refers to validity established by describing the content of a test or measurement procedure. For example, the content of a given algebra test could be specified in terms of the number of items dealing with fundamental operations, factoring, solving quadratic equations, exponentiation, and so on. Even better, an examination of the items themselves and their classification into content and process categories will give us an idea of the quality of the test in terms of its composition. The same may be true for any other kind of test. In effect, this procedure allows us to judge the meaningfulness of the test by examining its parts. Some advantages as well as disadvantages of this type of validity are evident. One advantage is the directness of the evidence to the question of validity. That is, the content and the test behaviors are directly judged as to their relevance for some purpose. This type of validity tends to have an impact when the test is being constructed. In fact, in most cases, test constructors work with a table of specifications which controls the content of the test during construction. To the degree that the specifications are valid and that items can be written faithfully for them, the test being developed will be valid by definition. For obvious reasons, this method is particularly effective with achievement tests in well-structured content areas. The weaknesses of content validity become evident where judgment is less sure. What, for example, should be the content of tests of creativity? Or personality? Or, for that matter, literature? Few of us feel that we are qualified to say. Those who do are often characterized more by their disagreement with others regarding content than by their agreement.

A second class of validity is that established by relating the test or procedure to criteria of one kind or another. Here, of course, there is frequently less than concensus regarding the appropriateness of the selected criterion. Usually, judgment is employed in the selection of either available or attainable criteria. This is followed by a determination of the relationship between the test to be validated and the selected criterion. Examples of criteria commonly used are: (1) tests similar to the test to be validated; (2) teacher or other judges' ratings of the trait measured by the test to be validated; and (3) demonstration of the trait measured in some context independent of the test being validated. Once the selection of a reasonable criterion is made, then measures are obtained from the test (X) and the criterion (Y), and some index of relationship, such as r or ρ, is determined. Here we would note that not only is the validity of X in question, but the quality of X's validity will be a function of the relevance of Y and the representativeness of the group from which the index of relationship is determined. The resolution of these issues is not an easy matter. The issues do suggest that assessing validity is a more complex problem than simply determining which test has the highest validity coefficient (r). As was suggested in the discussion of correlation coefficients, their size can also be influenced by the variability and accuracy of the measures. These influences further cloud the value of validity evidence based upon relationships with criteria. To summarize the problem, we may say that the validity of a test may be either overestimated or underestimated for a particular purpose. The size of a reported validity coefficient is useful evidence, but cannot be meaningfully interpreted until we know something about (1) the criterion selected, (2) the accuracy of both the test and the criterion measures, and (3) the group from which the validity data was obtained.

A special case of empirical validity involving criteria is that which is known as predictive validity. Here, the criterion Y is always some measure available after the test measure X. Usually, the criterion is a measure we would wish to predict in its own right. Examples are grades to be earned, success or failure in a training program, or improvement of some skill with remediation. In this case, our interpretation of validity coefficients seems clearer since we will probably accept as being most valid for predictive purposes the test that relates most highly to the fixed criterion. The problems of interpretation suggested earlier still apply, however, even though we may maintain that the criterion is fixed.

What we have called experimental validity is based upon the evidence of an "experiment." Let us suppose we wish to validate an achievement test. One way to do so would be to administer the test to students who had been instructed and students who had not been instructed. We would hope that scores on the test would differentiate the groups in favor of those who had been instructed. Another possibility would be to administer the test both before and after training. Again, we would argue that a valid test should register, in terms of change, the improvement of most groups after instruction. Another possibility would be to arrange for an independent "expert," such as a fellow teacher, to determine the "highest" and "lowest" achievers in the area assessed by the test. Here again, we would expect the test to show significant differences between these groups. These are but three examples of an almost limitless number of possibilities. In each case, the primary purpose is to contrive an "experiment" that will clearly provide validity evidence in a form acceptable to other investigators.

One final word regarding validity. Validity is always specific to a particular test and in terms of the method used to obtain it. There is no *the validity* of any test. There are validity estimates which vary widely, not only in terms of their value, but also in terms of the contexts from which they were obtained. Because of this, one is well-advised to be cautious about comparing validities on the basis of coefficients alone.

Reliabilities

Just as there are several ways to operationalize validity, there are several ways to operationalize reliability. All of these reliability methods are based upon the strategy of determining two or more independent but comparable measures of the same thing. Various ways to relate the sets of presumably comparable measures into indices of self-agreement are then applied to yield coefficients of reliability. The various methods for doing this can be classified into types or classes of reliability estimates. Generally, there are three types which consist of (1) measuring with the same instrument on two or more occasions, (2) measuring on one occasion with two or more independent but equivalent instruments, and (3) measuring on one occasion with one instrument which provides part-scores that are held to be equivalent. The kinds of reliability estimates provided by these three types of methods are commonly referred to as stability, equivalency, and internal-consistency, respectively. Sometimes, the first two methods, stability and equivalency, are employed together. Again, as with criterion-related validity, once the procedure for obtaining comparable measures is established, then some index of agreement between the estimates, such as r, is computed. The r then becomes the reliability coefficient.

In order to understand important distinctions between the various types of reliabilities, we need to consider error in measurement. Let us assume that we are interested in measuring a specific trait, for instance, arithmetic achievement, for a particular group. In the final analysis, we are measuring the trait for individual pupils and then collecting data for the given set of pupils. Let us conceptualize an individual's estimate as X_i, his score, and consider the score as consisting of two components: the true value of the trait (T_i), and an error component (E_i). The relationship between these values is given as:

$$X_i = T_i + E_i \qquad (5.1)$$

Formula 5.1 is a succinct way of stating that any observed score, (X), is an estimate of the value of the true score, (T). Any difference between X and T requires a value other than zero for error (E). In other words, observed scores may overestimate or underestimate true scores as a function of error. If we assume that true scores are constant, then it becomes evident that comparable values of X_i which differ among themselves reflect the degree of error present. In studying reliability, it is our purpose to determine how much error is present. Another way to state it is to say that when we study reliability, we are determining how much confidence we may place in our observations.

At this point, the reader may wonder how or why there is any error associated with measurement. We can identify three general sources of error in educational measurement which will help clarify the point. First, there is examinee or pupil-centered error. We all have our "good" and "bad" days. Sometimes, we are extraordinarily efficient or "sharp." That is, we perform beyond our customary ability. It is quite conceivable that, under these conditions, our performance is not typical, but rather, it overestimates our achievement. On the other hand, we have days when our performance is too low to be characteristic. Transitory moods, emotions, physical condition, rest, diet, and a host of personal factors can thus introduce error through the examinee himself. Second, the test instrument (or measurement procedure) may represent sources of error. All of us have experienced taking tests where either just the right things or just the wrong things were required. If we recognize that tests are only samples of behavior, we can see that the choice of items (sampling error) may be either to our advantage or to our disadvantage. Third, there are factors in the measurement situation which may introduce error. For example, uncomfortable seating, improper lighting, noise and distractions, the test administrator's behavior, and other situational factors can introduce error.

It is apparent, after we consider the various sources of error, that the procedures used to estimate reliability will differ with regard to the sources of error accounted for in the estimate. For example, if we correlate the scores of pupils obtained on two occasions using the *same* test, examinee-centered error but not instrument-centered error will be reflected in r. We must remember that we are interested in an honest estimation of reliability, not in spuriously favorable estimates. Generally speaking, the most comprehensive reliability coefficients with respect to error are those based upon equivalent forms taken on two occasions. Coefficients obtained under these conditions reflect error from all three sources that have been suggested. As one might expect, such coefficients are comparatively low and are more trouble to obtain than are other types. Table 16 presents a summary of the various kinds of coefficients, how they are obtained, the sources of error they "account for," and representative coefficients from selected tests.

TABLE 16

Summary of Types of Reliability Coefficients, Their Procedures,
Error Sources, and Representative Test Reliabilities

Type of Coefficient	How Obtained	Sources of Error "Accounted" For	Representative Coefficients and Test
1. Stability	Retest with One Form on Two or More Occasions	Situational and Personal Error	r = .91 (one year time), Elementary Level (grades 4-5) California Achievement Test; *Tech. Report on the California Achievement Tests*, Monterey: 1967.
2. Equivalence	Two or More Comparable Forms on One Occasion	Instrument-Centered Error (Item Sampling)	r = .95 (split-half corrected) grade 11, Madden-Peak Arithmetic Computation Tests, New York: Harcourt, Brace & World: 1956.
3. Stability and Equivalence	Two or More Forms on Two or More Occasions	Instrument-Centered, Situational, and Personal Errors	r = .90 (one week time) grade 8, Madden-Peak Arithmetic Computation Test, New York: Harcourt, Brace & World: 1956.
4. Internal-Consistency	Split-Half, Kuder-Richardson	Instrument-Centered Error	K-R 21: r = .97, grade 5, Elementary Level, California Achievement Test; *Tech. Report on the California Achievement Tests*, Monterey: 1967.

Standard Error of Measurement

An important construct in measurement which is directly related to reliability is the standard error of measurement (S.E.$_{meas.}$). The reader is familiar with the idea of S.E. $_{meas.}$ if he is familiar with physical measurement reported with tolerance limits. For example, machine parts are often described as some number of inches ± some limits, suggesting that the part has a known probability of falling between those limits. A piston head may be reported as having a diameter of 3″ ± .01″, meaning that, with specified probability, the piston's diameter is between 2.99″ and 3.01″. The ± limits suggest the precision with which the piston was machined. In the same way, S.E. $_{meas.}$ suggests the limits of accuracy for an observed score. Using a theoretically logical definition of reliability and certain assumptions, psychometricians have shown that the standard error of measurement is:

$$S.E._{meas.} = s \sqrt{1 - r} \text{, where} \tag{5.2}$$
$$s = \text{standard deviation of the test}$$
$$r = \text{reliability coefficient of the test.}$$

From (5.2), we may see that, if the reliability of a test is perfect (r = 1.00), that is, the measures are error free, S.E.$_{meas.}$ would be zero. In contrast, if the reliability of a test were zero (everything observed is in error), the S.E.$_{meas.}$ would be equal to the standard deviation of the test. Without undue detail for our purposes, let us say that, given an individual's obtained score, the generally accepted probability that his true score will be within one S.E.$_{meas.}$ of that value is 2/3. We may say that:

$$X_i \pm S.E._{meas.} \tag{5.3}$$

expresses a band of values for the individual's true score, with a probability of "correctness" equal to 2/3. Let us suppose, for example, that a given intelligence test had a reliability coefficient pertaining to I.Q. scores of .91. Further, the I.Q. score distribution has a standard deviation of 16. Applying formula (5.2), we would estimate the standard error of measurement to be:

$$\begin{aligned} S.E._{meas.} &= 16\sqrt{1-.91} \\ &= 16\sqrt{.09} \\ &= 16\cdot.3 \\ &= 5.4 \end{aligned}$$

Also, let us suppose that a given child's I.Q. is 100 as obtained on the same test. By formula (5.3), we may say (in the long run) that the chances are 2 out of 3 that the child's true I.Q. is between 94.6 and 105.4. Thus, we may see through the above formulas and example that the more reliable a given test, the more confidence we may place in obtained scores. It is important to note in this context that all measurement has error. Our purpose should be to try to estimate the amount of error in given situations in order to avoid unwarranted dogmatism regarding our data.

Classroom Tests

The concepts of reliability and validity are, of course, applicable to classroom tests and other kinds of informal measurement procedures. There are numerous techniques which have been developed to aid in improving such measurement. We shall discuss some of these techniques which have proven, through experience, to be useful.

Generally, the most useful way to deal with the problem of classroom test validity is through content analysis. It seems reasonable to assume that the teacher himself, by virtue of his command of subject matter and his knowledge of pupils, is in the best position to judge the validity of his own tests. Of course, teachers can be biased with respect to their own tests and abilities. They can also be guilty of careless test-construction and unsystematic appraisal. One way that these faults can be controlled is to build tests from content specifications. The procedure is to list the instructional objectives which should pay dividends both in instruction and in appraisal. Items for the test are then written in relation to the objectives and the course content. By thus controlling the test content, tests with reasonable content validiy should be assumed. A guide such as Bloom's *Taxonomy* can be of great help in developing items that call for significant educational behaviors. Another practical and useful technique is to ask for test critiques from teachers who are qualified to comment upon the subject matter and who are familiar with the pupils.

In a technical sense, following the recommendations for test construction which were provided earlier will pay off in improved reliability. To the degree that tests are valid in content, are of reasonable length, are free of ambiguous items, and are of appropriate difficulty, they will be technically sound. These general requirements influence both the validity and the reliability of tests in specific ways.

We have discussed content validity and have considered a general method for its control. The next requirement, reasonable test length, has its effect upon both validity (adequacy of content sampling) and reliability. That classroom tests are often too short to achieve acceptable reliability can be shown by the Spearman-Brown formula for estimating the reliability of "lengthened" tests. A common application of this formula is to estimate the reliability of tests by the "split-half" method. This procedure is to consider that a test consists of two equivalent halves, to score each half for each examinee, and then to correlate the scores between halves as an index of internal consistency. When all, or almost all, examinees finish all items on the test, a reasonable way to split the test is to score the odd and even numbered items as the half-tests. This procedure usually results in fairly equivalent halves. If, however, significant numbers of pupils do not finish the test, the last part of each half-test (the unattempted items) results in spurious agreement by virtue of the consistent failure over large parts of each half. This condition leads to overestimation of the test's reliability. Once the two halves are scored for each examinee, then the procedures for computing r or ρ as an estimate of r (which were given in Chapter 3) can be followed to obtain an index of agreement between the halves. Actually, this r can be considered to be an equivalent form reliability coefficient, but it is appropriate to a one-half length test. To correct that estimate by changing it to a coefficient appropriate to the full-length test, the Spearman-Brown formula is given as:

$$r_l = \frac{2r_{1/2}}{r_{1/2} + 1}, \text{ where} \tag{5.4}$$

r_l = the reliability of the full-length test.

$r_{1/2}$ = the correlation between the half-length tests.

To illustrate, if the scores for the odd and even numbered items on a test were determined to correlate at .60, then the reliability of the full-length test would be estimated by formula (5.4) to be:

$$r_l = \frac{2(.6)}{.6 + 1} = .75$$

There is available for this formula a generalized version which is appropriate for the estimation of tests lengthened (tripled, quadrupled, etc.) by any factor. In general, this formula suggests that the longer the tests become, the more reliable they are. There is at least one catch to this generalization. It assumes that the quality of the items in the lengthened test is comparable to the quality of the original items. Whether or not item writers can maintain a given quality of item over increasing test length is an interesting question. In any case, the important point regarding test length is that both theory and experience demonstrate that short tests are usually less reliable than long tests. In classroom use, it is advisable to base important evaluations upon long-term observations and composite measures in order to gain the reliability that educational decisions require.

To further enhance the reliability of tests, items must be as free of ambiguity as possible. Further, items should contain a central problem or point which can clearly be scored, that is, for which there is a defensible correct answer. Items lacking clear answers or which are ambiguous invite chance responses. When responses are, in part, based upon chance, the reliability of the test decreases accordingly.

A related problem in test construction is the inclusion of items of inappropriate difficulty. Let us suppose, for example, that in a given test, a certain item is so difficult that all, or nearly all, respondents fail to answer it correctly. In effect, the item results in a constant (0) being added to each examinee's score. Such items shorten the effective length of the test in equivalence to their number. In other words, as far as making distinctions among examinees in terms of achievement (or any other trait), these items add nothing. The same may be said of items which are so easy that all examinees answer correctly. In spite of their great therapeutic value, these items do not add to information designed to make distinctions among pupils of differing achievement. This discussion leads us to a final practical procedure for evaluating tests themselves. The procedure is called item analysis, and it can help us assess both the reliability and the validity of our classroom tests.

Item Analysis

   Item analysis is based upon two characteristics of items. They are the discrimination and the difficulty values of the items as determined by empirical count of the examinee responses to individual items. It has already been suggested that items which are either too difficult or too easy are inefficient in terms of their contribution to total test scores. For this reason, it is desirable to determine those items which should either be discarded or revised in future test use because of inappropriate difficulty levels. In addition to this, it is highly desirable to determine those items which are most useful in differentiating between pupils of relatively high achievement and those of relatively low achievement. In short, and as we shall see, items which discriminate between levels of achievement will necessarily be of sufficient difficulty to accomplish that end.

   In order to understand the rationale for methods of item analysis, we first need to consider the establishment of what we will refer to as criterion groups. If we knew, independent of our tests, which pupils possessed the trait measured by the test and which did not, we would expect a valid test to yield relatively high scores for the first group and relatively low scores for the second. In the case of achievement, we would hold that those with greater achievement should have significantly higher scores than those with lesser achievement. To illustrate, let us suppose that we have two pupils, A and B, with A having greater achievement than B. Also let us suppose that we devise a six-item test to measure that achievement, and that the following data indicate the performance of pupils A and B, item by item. Plus indicates correct, and minus indicates incorrect.

Item No.	Pupil:	A	B
1		+	−
2		+	+
3		−	−
4		+	−
5		+	+
6		−	+

Now we can see that the total score for A will be 4 and is greater than the total score for B which is 3. But how do the individual items perform in terms of contributing to the distinction? We can tell by inspection of the responses that items 1 and 4 differentiated in the desired direction, that is, A+ and B−. Items 3 and 5 are ineffective in that both A and B performed in the same ways on them, that is, both missed item 3, and both were correct on item 5. Finally, item 6 differentiates, but to our horror, in a direction opposite to that we would like, that is, B, the lower achiever, answered correctly, and A, the "star," missed it. The purpose of this simple example is to illustrate how item "counts" can be utilized to review the efficiency of items. The strategy has been developed so that a great deal of useful test information can be derived on the basis of item analysis.

To develop the techniques of item analysis further, we need to consider the problem of establishing the criterion groups used to determine the discrimination power of the items. Usually, we cannot or do not know those examinees who possess more achievement or less achievement. Sometimes, it is possible to constitute criterion groups on the basis of external evidence, such as prior course grades, intelligence, and so forth, but usually the most practical procedure is to use evidence from the test which is being analyzed itself. That is, we can determine the necessary criterion groups on the basis of total test score, assuming that total scores differentiate examinees of varying achievement. For this purpose, we shall call high scorers the "hi" criterion group and low scorers the "lo" criterion group. To diagram the situation, let the following line represent the continuum of scores on a given test.

	Lo Group		Hi Group
X ———
Low Scores		Score Scale	High Scores

Our purpose will be to determine hi and lo criterion groups from the frequency distribution of scores on the total test. We will assume that groups so constituted provide meaningful contrast groups in terms of total achievement and thus provide valid evidence, item by item, for the analysis. The most contrasting groups we could constitute would be the pupil with the very highest total score vs. the pupil with the very lowest score. This procedure, however, would be wasteful in terms of the total amount of data available to us. We could, in order to incorporate as much data as possible, split the group in half at the middle. But this procedure provides weak contrasts between hi and lo groups around the center score. Various recommendations have been made to compromise the loss of data and clarity of contrast in defining criterion groups. Taking the top 25% vs. the bottom 25% is a method often used. Under certain theoretical assumptions, the two extreme 27%'s of the distribution can be shown to be the most valid compromise. In classroom test situations where the total n of the test's frequency distribution tends to be small, the usual practice is to obtain the largest hi-lo criterion groups possible without using tied scores at the center. A requirement of the method is that there be the same number in each criterion group. Let the following frequency distribution serve to illustrate:

X	f	cf
25	1	37
24	2	36
23	0	34
22	2	34
21	4	32
20	3	28
19	5	25
18	7	20
17	5	13
16	4	8
15	1	4
14	2	3
13	0	1
12	1	1
$n = 37$		

We note here that there is an n of 37 for the entire distribution. If we divide the sum of the frequencies by 2, we learn that 18.5 represents half the distribution. Thus, an ideal "break" for the two groups would be 18 in each, discarding the "center" pupil as being not clearly hi or lo. By inspection, we see that the 18 low scores include the 13 lowest values (12-17), plus 5 of the scores of 18. The 18 hi scores include the 17 scores from 19-25 and one of the scores of 18. To avoid duplicate scores in the two groups, we could make several decisions: (1) discard for item analysis three scores of 18 and define the hi group as the top 17 scores (19-25) and the lo group as the bottom 17 scores (12-18); (2) define the hi group as the top 12 scores (20-25) vs. the bottom 12 scores (12-17), discarding one score of 17 to gain equal numbers in the two groups; (3) define the hi and lo groups as the top and bottom 10 scores, respectively (hi: 20-25 one score of 20 taken to reach 10; lo: 12-17 two scores of 17 taken to reach 10); (4) any of a number of other decisions designed to identify an equal number of "hi" and "lo" pupils.

We will see that there is an advantage in picking groups of a size which lend themselves to easier computation, such as multiples of 5 or 10. For that reason, in our example, we will follow the third decision above, namely, top 10 vs. bottom 10. After this decision is made, we simply organize the test papers into two groups, the hi group and the lo group. Then for each item, we tally the number of examinees in each group who answered the item correctly. To illustrate, to the left of Table 17 are hypothetical counts for each of the criterion groups for the 25-item test of our example. We may now define and illustrate the two item analysis indices of interest for our purposes. The difficulty index is defined as:

$$\text{Diff.} = \frac{\#R_{hi} + \#R_{lo}}{n_{hi} + n_{lo}} \cdot 100, \text{ where} \tag{5.5}$$

$\#R_{hi}$ = the number of correct responses from the hi group.

$\#R_{lo}$ = the number of correct responses from the lo group.

n_{hi} = number of examinees in the hi group.

n_{lo} = number of examinees in the lo group.

Item Difficulty

The difficulty index is, by virtue of the multiplier 100, an estimate of the percent of all examinees answering the item correctly. Strictly

TABLE 17

Illustrative Item Analysis Data for a Twenty-five Item Test

	Tallies of Criterion Groups:		No. Correct:			
Item No.	Hi	Lo	Hi	Lo	Diff.	Discrim.
1	卌 卌	卌 ||	10	7	85	0.30
2	卌 ||||	||||	9	4	65	0.50
3	卌 卌	卌 |	10	6	80	0.40
4	卌	卌	5	5	50	0.00
5	卌 卌	卌 ||	10	7	85	0.30
6	卌 卌	卌 ||	10	7	85	0.30
7	卌 卌	卌 |||	10	8	90	0.20
8	卌 卌	卌 |||	10	8	90	0.20
9	卌 ||	||||	7	4	55	0.30
10	卌 卌	卌 卌	10	10	100	0.00
11	卌 |||	||||	8	4	60	0.40
12	卌 卌	卌 ||	10	7	85	0.30
13	卌 卌	卌 |||	10	8	90	0.20
14	卌 卌	卌 |	10	6	80	0.40
15	卌 |||	||||	8	4	60	0.40
16	卌 ||||	卌	9	5	70	0.40
17	卌 卌	卌 ||	10	7	85	0.30
18	卌 卌	卌	10	5	75	0.50
19	卌 |	||||	6	4	50	0.20
20	卌 卌	卌 ||	10	7	85	0.30
21	卌 卌	卌 |||	10	8	90	0.20
22	卌 卌	卌 |	10	6	80	0.40
23	卌 ||||	卌	9	5	70	0.40
24	|||	卌 |	3	6	45	-0.30
25	卌 ||	卌	7	5	60	0.20

speaking, it is inversely related to difficulty, as when all hi and lo examinees are correct, the index is 100, and when none is correct, the index is zero. To illustrate the application of formula (5.5) for the first two items of Table 17, we have:

Item 1: $\text{Diff.} = \dfrac{10 + 7}{10 + 10} \cdot 100 = \dfrac{17}{20} \cdot 100 = 85$

Item 2: $\text{Diff.} = \dfrac{9 + 4}{10 + 10} \cdot 100 = \dfrac{13}{20} \cdot 100 = 65$

We should bear in mind that the difficulty index is an empirical index based upon performance. It simply reports the difficulty in terms of percent correct. This percent is not necessarily related to the complexity or to the effort involved in the solution of the item. Nonetheless, it is a useful index in terms of identifying test items which are either efficient or inefficient. It can be shown that the 50% difficulty level is the ideal level in terms of delivering measurement information. If we scan the data of Table 17, we see two items, 4 and 19, with that value. In practice, difficulty levels between 20% and 80% are considered "keepers," and even items with values outside these limits are sometimes retained on the basis of uniqueness or content. Actually, hard and fast rules for item retention are less desirable than a recognition of the fact that 50% difficulty is an ideal to be strived for. Items which are inefficiently easy or difficult can often be revised "up" or "down," and item analysis can provide the information that allows rational improvement of the test. We will return to the index of difficulty as a means of estimating test reliability after we consider the index of discrimination.

Item Discrimination

The index of discrimination is defined as:

$$\text{Discrim.} = \frac{\#R_{hi} - \#R_{lo}}{n_{hi \text{ or } lo}}, \text{ where} \tag{5.6}$$

$\#R_{hi} =$ the number of correct responses from the hi group.

$\#R_{lo} =$ the number of correct responses from the lo group.

$n_{hi \text{ or } lo} =$ the number of examinees in either the hi or lo group.

The discrimination index gives the difference in correct responses between the criterion groups as a proportion of either group. We recall that $n_{hi} = n_{lo}$. Therefore, the difference of the numerator is reported as a proportion of the same denominator, whether hi or lo. Let us consider the possibilities for values of the index. If all the hi group and none of the lo group are correct, then $\frac{\#R_{hi} - \#R_{lo}}{n_{hi}}$ becomes $\frac{n_{hi} - 0}{n_{hi}}$ or 1.00. This value represents perfect discrimination for the item. If an equal number of hi and lo examinees is correct on any item, $\frac{\#R_{hi} - \#R_{lo}}{n_{hi}}$ becomes $\frac{0}{n_{hi}} = 0.0$. This value indicates no discriminating power for the item. It simply does not differentiate between those with presumably greater and those with presumably lesser achievement. If, for any item, there is a greater number of correct responses from the lo group than from the hi group, the index will be negative, with the extreme case being −1.00. That value indicates "no hi's, all lo's gaining the item," the symptom of a very faulty item. To illustrate the application of formula (5.6) for the first two items of Table 17, we have:

$$\text{Item 1:} \quad \text{Discrim.} = \frac{10 - 7}{10} = 0.30$$

$$\text{Item 2:} \quad \text{Discrim.} = \frac{9 - 4}{10} = 0.50$$

As with the difficulty index, the discrimination index provides a basis for evaluating items. Weak and negative discriminators can often be revised for their improvement and, of course, the general improvement of the test. The ideal discrimination value for an item is +1.00. In practice, the higher the better, but values of 0.40 and higher are usually quite acceptable. Again, we should remember that this is an empirical index, and there may be compelling content arguments for retaining items which should otherwise be discarded. The index is a useful way, however, to view validity at the item level.

Estimating Classroom Test Reliability

A useful formula for estimating the reliability of tests was developed for situations where the difficulty index for all items is available. Statisticians refer to the index of difficulty as p when it is given as a proportion rather than as a percent. Since the proportion for answering an item correctly plus the proportion for answering it incorrectly equals 1.00, it follows that $1 - p =$ the proportion incorrect. This proportion is called q, and the reliability estimate is based upon the pq products for all items. The formula is valid only if items are scored one point if correct and no point if incorrect. The statisticians who developed the formula are Kuder and Richardson[3] and the particular formula given here was formula 20 from their paper. It is widely accepted and is known as K-R 20. The formula is:

$$r_{\text{K-R 20}} = \frac{k}{k - 1}\left(1 - \frac{\Sigma pq}{s^2}\right) \text{ where} \tag{5.7}$$

$k =$ the number of items in the test.
$p =$ proportion correct for each item.
$q =$ proportion incorrect for each item.
$\Sigma pq =$ the sum for all items of the pq products.
$s^2 =$ the variance of the test scores.

To provide an illustration of the application of formula (5.7), the frequency distribution for the data of Table 17 is given again in Table 18 along with the item p and q values determined from the difficulty index column.

---

[3]G. F. Kuder, and M. W. Richardson, "The Theory of the Estimation of Test Reliability," *Psychometrica*, II, (Sept. 1937), pp. 151-160.

TABLE 18

Illustration of Computation of a Reliability Coefficient by K-R 20

Frequency Distribution of Test Scores						Test Item	p	q	pq
X	f	d	fd	fd^2					
25	1	7	7	49		1	.85	.15	.1275
						2	.65	.35	.2275
24	2	6	12	72		3	.80	.20	.1600
						4	.50	.50	.2500
23	0	5	0	0		5	.85	.15	.1275
						6	.85	.15	.1275
22	2	4	8	32		7	.90	.10	.0900
						8	.90	.10	.0900
21	4	3	12	36		9	.55	.45	.2475
						10	1.00	.00	.0000
20	3	2	6	12		11	.60	.40	.2400
						12	.85	.15	.1275
19	5	1	5	5		13	.90	.10	.0900
						14	.80	.20	.1600
18	7	0	0	0		15	.60	.40	.2400
						16	.70	.30	.2100
17	5	-1	-5	5		17	.85	.15	.1275
						18	.75	.25	.1875
16	4	-2	-8	16		19	.50	.50	.2500
						20	.85	.15	.1275
15	1	-3	-3	9		21	.90	.10	.0900
						22	.80	.20	.1600
14	2	-4	-8	32		23	.70	.30	.2100
						24	.45	.55	.2475
13	0	-5	0	0		25	.60	.40	.2400
12	1	-6	-6	36				Σpq	= 4.1550

$$\Sigma fd = 1 \quad \Sigma fd^2 = 304$$

In order to utilize formula (5.7), we need to determine the Σpq and s^2 values for our data. Applying formula (3.14) to the data of Table 18, the variance is:

$$s^2 = i^2 \left[\frac{\Sigma fd^2}{N} - \left(\frac{\Sigma fd}{N}\right)^2 \right]$$
$$= i^2 \left[\frac{304}{37} - \left(\frac{1}{37}\right)^2 \right]$$
$$= 1 \ [8.2162 - .0007]$$
$$= \quad 8.2155 \text{ or } 8.22$$

The Σpq value as determined from Table 18 is 4.1550. Thus, the application of formula (5.7) to our data is:

$$r_{\text{K-R 20}} = \frac{k}{k-1}\left(1 - \frac{\Sigma pq}{s^2}\right)$$

$$= \frac{25}{24}\left(1 - \frac{4.155}{8.22}\right)$$

$$= 1.04\ (1 - .505)$$

$$= 1.04\ (\ .495)$$

$$= .51$$

The obtained coefficient suggests less reliability than we would like in most situations. It should be remembered that short tests usually tend to be unstable. This fact suggests one obvious approach to the improvement of the illustrative test. If 10 to 15 items are added, improvement should take place. Also, if we review the item difficulty levels, we note that, by and large, the items are easy. The lowest difficulty index is 45 for item 24. Too many of the items are at the levels 80 and above. Some improvement should result from revision and replacement of these items in an effort to develop a somewhat more difficult form.

One other and simpler means of estimating reliability will be given. Kuder and Richardson developed, under a different set of assumptions, the following reliability estimate which became known as K-R 21. It is:

$$r_{\text{K-R 21}} = \frac{k}{k-1}\left[1 - \frac{\overline{X}\left(1 - \frac{\overline{X}}{k}\right)}{s^2}\right], \text{ where} \qquad (5.8)$$

k = number of items in the test.

$\overline{X}$ = the mean of the test scores.

s^2 = the variance of the test scores.

To apply formula (5.8) to the data of Table 18 requires only the mean and variance of the distribution. These statistics, ($\overline{X}$ and s^2), are normally desired anyway; therefore, getting the K-R 21 reliability estimate is a small additional step. Using (5.8) for our illustration, then, requires the computation of the mean only, since we have previously computed the variance. Applying formula (3.6) to obtain the mean, we have from Table 18:

$$\overline{X}_d = i\left(\frac{\Sigma fd}{N}\right) + \text{A.R.}$$

$$= 1\left(\frac{1}{37}\right) + 18$$

$$= 0.027 + 18$$

$$= 18.027$$

Recalling that $s^2 = 8.22$ from the same data by application of (3.14), we have for (5.8):

$$
\begin{aligned}
r_{\text{K-R 21}} &= \frac{25}{24}\left[1 - \frac{18.027\left(1 - \frac{18.027}{25}\right)}{8.22}\right] \\
&= 1.04\left[1 - \frac{18.027\,(1 - 0.721)}{8.22}\right] \\
&= 1.04\left[1 - \frac{18.027\,(0.279)}{8.22}\right] \\
&= 1.04\left[1 - \frac{5.03}{8.22}\right] \\
&= 1.04\,[1 - 0.612] \\
&= 1.04\,[0.388] \\
&= 0.40
\end{aligned}
$$

As we can see, this estimate is even smaller than the earlier one from K-R 20. One of the statistical assumptions for K-R 21 is that the difficulty levels of the items are equal. This assumption is violated, of course, in most classroom tests. The effect of departure from the various assumptions of the formula is to yield underestimates of test reliability. For this reason, K-R 21 is often taken to be a minimum estimate of any test's reliability. The main advantage of K-R 21 is that it is relatively easy to determine, requiring as it does the computation of only the mean and the variance.

Concluding Comments

We have dealt with some of the issues, logic, history, and techniques of evaluation and measurement in education. Our approach has been through discussion, illustration, and application. The treatment presented here is necessarily selective and abridged. The serious student of evaluation will wish to pursue the many facets of the subject further. In this pursuit, he will find that there are no cut and dried answers to the problems and issues raised. Rather, he will find that the further he goes, the more interesting and complex will the task become. In the final analysis, educational evaluation is as complex and comprehensive as education itself. We as educators must make the first steps in evaluation as rationally as possible. The effort, like instruction itself, becomes self-perpetuating and is equally challenging and rewarding. The important thing is to make the first step with the ultimate purpose of improving educational opportunities for all.

Additional Reading

Adams, Georgia S. *Measurement and Evaluation in Education, Psychology, and Guidance.* New York: Holt, Rinehart & Winston, 1964.
An introductory text of unusual sophistication. Pointed to both teachers and counselors, and very complete.

Thorndike, R. L., and Hagen, Elizabeth. *Measurement and Evaluation in Psychology and Education,* 3d ed. New York: John Wiley & Sons, 1969.
An excellent revision of an older classic. A wealth of information on theory and technique for the effective design and use of educational measurement.

Index

abscissa, 46
Adams, G. S., 115
Anastasi, A., 36
asymmetrical distributions, 48
averages, 53-58

behaviorism, 3
Binet, A., 19
Bloom, B. S., 4, 87, 88, 89, 96
Boring, E. G., 23
Buros, O. K., 96, 98

Chase, C. J., 24
Chauncey, H., 15, 19, 24
Commission on Science Education, 4, 5
completion tests, 92-93
content validity, 99
continuous variables, 41
correlations, 73-81
  interpretation of, 76, 78-81
  Pearson product-moment, 75-77
  rho, 77-78
criterion related validity, 99-101
Cronbach, L. J., 36
cumulative frequencies, 44

Diederich, P. B., 81
difficulty index, 109
discrete variables, 40-41
discrimination index, 111
Dobbin, J. E., 15, 19, 24

Ebel, R. L., 96
education
  purposes, 1-2, 82-84
  scope of, 1
Edwards, A. L., 81
emotional objectives, 87
empirical validity, 99-101
empiricism, 26-28
Englehart, M. D., 88, 96
entering behavior, 83-84
essay tests, 91-92
evaluation, 7-10
  history of, 14-24
  perspective, 14
  purposes, 29
  related to teaching and learning, 82-84
experimental validity, 100

Findley, W. G., 24
frequency distributions, 38-52
  grouped, 42-45
  interval, 43
frequency polygons, 46-47
Furst, E. J., 9, 88, 96

Glaser, R., 83
graphical representation, 45-52
Guilford, J. P., 21, 31

Hagen, E., 116
Helmstadter, G. C., 36
Hill, W. H., 88, 96

histograms, 46-47
Hoffman, B., 13, 24
Horrocks, J. E., 17
Huff, D., 13

integral limits, 43
intellectual objectives, 86-87
isomorphism, 31
item analysis, 107-112
    difficulty index, 109-111
    discrimination index, 111-112

Joint Committee on Testing, 13

Katz, M., 96
Kelly, T. L., 17
knowledge, 26-27
Krathwohl, D. R., 87, 88, 89, 96
Kuder-Richardson formula #20, 112
Kuder-Richardson formula #21, 114
kurtosis, 49

learning, 83
Lindquist, E. F., 81
Lindvall, C. M., 36, 84
Ludlow, H. G., 24

Mager, R. F., 85, 96
Mann, H., 16
Masia, B. B., 4, 87, 89
mean, 54-58
measurement, 7-8
    educational, 28-30
    related to instruction and
        evaluation, 83-84
    standardized, 15-16
median, 58
mode, 48
multiple-choice tests, 94-96

New York City School's Grade Guide,
    5-6
Noll, V. H., 7
normal curve, 51-53
numbers, 30
numerals, 31

objectives
    general, 2, 6
    intermediate, 2, 4-6
    related to teaching and learning,
        83-84
    specific, 2, 6-7, 84-86
    taxonomies of, 4

ultimate, 3-4
ogives, 46-47
ordinate, 46

percentile ranks, 59-62
percentiles, 63-65
physical-motor objectives, 87-89

real limits, 43
Reech, G. M., 17
relative frequencies, 45
reliability, 97, 101-103
    classroom tests, 104-106, 112-115
    equivalence, 101-103
    internal consistency, 101-103,
        112-115
    stability, 101-103
Rice, J. M., 16-17

scales, 30
    four types, 32-36
Schoer, L. A., 81
Schoonover, T., 17
scientific method, 27
semi-interquartile range, 66
skewness, 49
social objectives, 87-89
Spearman-Brown formula, 106
standard deviation, 69, 70
standard error of measurement,
    103-104
standard scores, 72-73
Standards for Educational and
    Psychological Tests, 98
statistical methods, history of, 21-24
statistics, descriptive and inferential,
    37-38
Stevens, S. S., 7, 30
symmetrical distributions, 48

teaching, 83
Terman, L. M., 17
test information, 98
testing, 7, 8
    critics' views, 13-14
    educational, history of, 16-18
    forms of, 90-96
    intelligence, 19-21
    proponents' views, 10-12
    psychological, history of, 18-21
tests, standardized, 98
Thorndike, E. L., 10, 11, 17
Thorndike, R. L., 116

Tinkelman, S. N., 94
true-false tests, 93-94

validity, 97, 98-101
    classroom tests, 104-106

Van Dalen, D. B., 26
variability, 65-72
variance, 68-69, 70

Wernick, R., 13